A Memoir

MY LAST BAGGAGE CALL
ABOARD AIR FORCE ONE

A Journey of Sacrifice, Service, Family, and Friendship

To Cecil

THAnk you For

your support

D1523116

Writing Our World Publishing
2 Rosier Court
Little Rock, Arkansas 72211

My Last Baggage Call Aboard Air Force One: Recounting a Journey of Sacrifice, Service, Family, and Friendship by Sergeant First Class (Retired) Glenn W. Powell

Books may be purchased by contacting the publisher:

Writing Our World Publishing
2 Rosier Court
Little Rock, Arkansas 72211
www.wowpublishing.org

Cover Design: Melanie Jones
Creative Consultant: L. Marie LLC
ISBN: 9 7809889644 33

Library of Congress Control Number: 2016912920
1. Memoir 2. Political
First Edition
Printed in United States

Ordering Information:

Special discounts are available on quantity purchases by churches, nonprofits, and other organizations. For details, contact the publisher at the address above.

What others are saying about

Sergeant First Class (Retired) Glenn W. Powell

"Although most know Glenn Powell as a military man, I know him as one of America's best diplomats. He traveled the world countless times and always represented our country with great distinction. I consider myself fortunate to have had the opportunity to work with him for many years during my tenure as US Ambassador to the United Nations and as Secretary of State."
—Secretary of State, Madeleine K. Albright

"Glenn Powell achieves a rare feat in writing poignantly of an America that still holds hope for those who dare to reach for it. He balances his story of growing up in the urban north in the 1960s with the years when we met, both living our dreams as members of the White House staff in the 1990s. Through it all, and to a great extent, because of it all, Glenn Powell's message is one of hope."—Congressman Sean Maloney, D-NY

"Glenn Powell's memoir is a story of one young man's journey that resulted in the American Dream. His book honors the US Military, military families, and all of the men and women who devote their lives to public service. *My Last Baggage Call* is a message of possibilities—that sacrifice with purpose can and should lead to success."—Terry McAuliffe, Governor of VA

"Sergeant Powell, this day (your retirement) is a momentous one for the army and you. For almost thirty years, the army has been a member of your family and you, its. This thirty-year relationship has taken you from New Jersey to Texas to Virginia to the White House. And, I have no doubt that you completed each of your assignments with commitment, consummate skill, and dignity." —The Honorable Vernon Jordan

"Glenn has a natural and proven ability to make any endeavor or business better than what they are. He is a contributor and doer with high energy and he knows how to channel that energy in whatever he does. If he's interested, he's thought about it completely through before taking action. I think it is interesting that Glenn served under both Bushes, as well as President Clinton."

—Ambassador Thomas F. "Mack" McLarty

Dedication

This book is dedicated to my parents George Bowman and Margaret Powell. You set the foundation on which my whole life is built. Your constant support and love have always given me the strength that I needed to be successful.

I would also like to dedicate this book to Command Sergeant Major (Retired) Fletcher Walker and Sergeant First Class (Retired) David Horn. You both played a vital role during my military career. Not only did you provide me with the necessary tools to succeed as I rose through the ranks, but you also provided me with the tools to become the man that I am today. Your mentorship and friendship meant more to me than you will ever know. Even though you are no longer here, we were and always will be family, and I know that you are always watching over me with pride.

Acknowledgment

There are so many individuals that have made this dream of telling my story a reality. I have had this idea for a long time, and I wanted to tell my story while I could. So many people depart this world without sharing their amazing life journeys with others. I didn't want to be one of them.

I truly appreciate the many family, friends, coworkers, and peers that took time out of their busy schedules to share their adventures and sentiments with and about me. Just know that my journey and experiences with you will forever bind us together.

Table of Contents

A Photo Journey (pgs. 87 - 112)

Your life is not important except how it impacts others.

—Jackie Robinson

Foreword

My life, especially my adult life, has revolved around the military. I am so proud of the honor of serving my country. My most exciting assignments were overseas in Europe where I commanded at the company, battalion, and brigade levels. As the Commander of the 2nd Signal Brigade, I supervised 2500 soldiers and civilians dispersed throughout Europe including England, Germany, the Netherlands, Belgium, and Italy.

I was serving as Commander of the 2nd Signal Brigade in Europe when I received a call from the White House Military Office (WHMO) about interviewing for the position of Commander of the White House Communications Agency. My initial interview took place at the White House Communications Agency Headquarters at the Naval Support Facility Anacostia in Washington, D.C. with Commander Colonel Thomas Hawes. My final interview was with Mr. Al Maldon, deputy assistant to the president and director of the White House Military Office.

I was offered the job and accepted it. I was flattered to learn later that Mr. Leroy Borden, one of the longest serving and most respected directors of the White House Transportation Agency had weighed in on the final decision to hire me. Mr. Borden had known my father during the Reagan and Bush Administrations, and suggested to Mr. Maldon that, "If the son is one-tenth as good as his father, he is the man for the job."

However, it wouldn't take me long to realize that I had my work cut out for me. I would need a top-notch person to help me navigate the White House Communications Office. There were lots of things I just didn't know about the White House operations, like where I sat on AF1, and what the term CARPET meant.

Enter Sergeant First Class Glenn Powell. Meeting Glenn was a Godsend for several reasons. First and foremost, he helped me navigate through this challenging and chaotic time. It was very comforting to have someone like Glenn there to answer questions and develop a relationship. Anytime I was on AF1, Glenn was right there. Thank God! Just as importantly, Glenn's wife, Ronda, was working in the Department of Defense at the time. After talking with Glenn, I realized Ronda would be perfect for the executive assistant administrative position I needed to fill...someone to help me straighten out my office.

In time, I learned that Glenn had a real ability to connect and communicate with others, and he genuinely cares about others. He is a team player who adapts when he needs to or finds a way to contribute. Administratively and logistically, he is top-notch, accountable, loyal, responsible, and trustworthy. He has strong intuition and is highly observant. Unlike most of us, Glenn doesn't hesitate to ask questions if he doesn't understand something.

I greatly admired Glenn's reverence for family. His family is paramount to him, and he always found joy in his faith and in helping others. He has his priorities straight. After meeting his mother, I realized where that came from. Glenn grew up in a family where making a difference was important and there were high expectations about what you do with the opportunities given to you. While Glenn is ambitious, he integrates it with this wonderfully wry sense of humor and an incredible work ethic. Beyond his ambition, he is a team-builder who led his group with integrity. They all looked up to him.

When I became WHMO director, I made it a point to be a part of the CARPET (White House Transportation) exercises. The president was traveling to Aspen and I made a point of shadowing Glenn to experience the job his team did transferring luggage on and off AF1 to the hotels or homes. It was edifying to see what these guys did from 3:00 to 4:00 in the mornings. I was whipped but had a greater appreciation for the roles they played in the whole scheme of things. Glenn always took his job very seriously. I don't think most people knew what all went into taking care of AF1 passengers.

I can truthfully say that I probably survived my trip to Jakarta, Indonesia, thanks to Ronda's chicken wings. One of the president's trips during his last term was to Jakarta, and it was so hot I could barely breathe. It was absolutely miserable. Glenn knew I was always tentative about eating in foreign countries. My wife would pack my stuff and I would preach to my troops about watching what they ate. I knew that nothing was going to happen to Glenn because Ronda would prepare delicious chicken wings that Glenn eventually shared with me. I survived many foreign trips thanks to Ronda's chicken wings.

Glenn was both daring and courageous, and he always sought new adventures and new challenges. He was also humble, not prone to bragging about his accomplishments. His trust in others inspired loyalty from his team. His sense of responsibility and accountability were attributes that surely evolved over a lifetime and benefitted him greatly in his journey. Those of us who worked with him knew that when AF1 landed, the livelihoods of the people on that plane depended to a great extent on Glenn Powell.

The Honorable Joseph J. (Jake) Simmons, IV
Former Director, White House Military Office
and the Former White House
Communications Agency Commander,
Clinton Administration

Introduction

I am from Toledo, Ohio, born and bred. "Rust Belt" country. However, in preparing to write this memoir spanning my twenty years of military service, eleven of which included assignments in the White House, I learned that my past inextricably connects to Arkansas. Maybe I should have called this book *From the Rust Belt to the White House by Way of Arkansas.*

Growing up in Ohio in the 1960s, I knew almost nothing about Arkansas. My ignorance did not keep me, a northerner, from looking down on the state and southerners in general as a backward people with a depressing backstory. Today, I can honestly say that out of all of my White House assignments, the best was serving as logistics operator aboard AF1 under a favorite son of Arkansas—President William J. Clinton—who was without question one of the most forward-thinking presidents this nation has ever produced.

Ironically, throughout my life more folks than I can count have mistaken *me* as a southerner. My soft-spoken, laid-back demeanor and big smile fooled them every time. However, when we became more acquainted, the "Toledo" in me came out. Even when I left Ohio in 1982 to join the army, my new acquaintances pegged me as 'that super nice guy' – probably from the south. "I'm from Toledo, Ohio!" I would decry, with more than a little attitude. Most of them would respond, "Toledo…where is *that?*" They were nearly as ignorant about my Rust Belt origins as I was about the southern Bible Belt. They had the basic inkling that culturally, Ohio was a long way from the south and harvesting corn, cotton, and soybean. I would explain to them that Toledo's claim to fame was creating glass and steel products, manufacturing cars, and mining oil.

Looking back, I can see how that would be underwhelming to my twenty-something year-old peers. No matter how I dressed it up, Toledo wasn't Cincinnati, Ohio with its major league baseball team and professional football team, not to mention the city's respected Underground Railroad history. Toledo wasn't Cleveland, Ohio either with more professional sports teams than Cincinnati, not to mention employing the first African American mayor to run a big city in the United States—Carl Burton Stokes.

Despite what Toledo was not, there was more to it than I realized and I needed to know about it. I knew of African American outmigration from the south to the north. African American communities were popping up all over the north filled with families seeking living conditions beyond cotton fields, educational roadblocks, and blatant, pervasive discrimination that kept them uneducated, unemployed, underemployed, poor, and living in fear. Even Toledo promised a better life, though I can imagine the culture shock of factories and mills. The financial tradeoffs, if nothing else, had to make the migration to the north worth it. My search to learn more about Toledo (as many searches of this sort often will) led me to dig deeper into my personal family origins. I discovered Scottish and West Indies ancestors, and I discovered, of all things, my Arkansas lineage.

When I retired from the military and the White House in 2002, I had served three United States Presidents: George H. W. Bush, William J. Clinton, and George W. Bush. While it was an honor to serve in each administration, the Clinton administration felt most like...well, most like a union—dare I say a *re*union—between the best ideas and intentions of north and south, and each region of the United States. From advisors, to chauffeurs to cooks to cabinet members, and every role in between, African Americans were included in the Clinton White House. The opportunities that the Clinton Administration extended to minorities were not unlike the opportunities southern Blacks had found in the north. The Clinton Administration was a rarified climate, and people worldwide wanted to breathe the air at 1600 Pennsylvania Avenue between 1992 and 2000.

Once in a lifetime experiences were the trademark of my service during that time. I experienced African Safaris, the Australian Outback, the Great Wall of China, Red Square, the Pyramids of Egypt, the Russian Kremlin, Tiananmen Square, and more. During the making of the movie, *Air Force One*, I met actor Harrison Ford, and attended the screening of the film in California with President Clinton as a member of his entourage.

I met television host Arsenio Hall around the time Mr. Clinton was a presidential candidate and guest on the Late Show, where he dunned dark shades and played the saxophone. I met Chris Tucker when he was preparing to star in a movie as the US President. I met the incomparable opera star Jessye Norman, Run DMC, actor Bruce Willis, singer Carly Simon, and Carol Channing. A super nice, practical woman, Ms. Channing asked me to drive her to Tysons Corner Mall because she had forgotten her best bras back home. I met news reporter, Connie Chung, and forged a lasting friendship with her.

The chance to interface with the president's family on a regular basis was exciting too. The first lady's mother, Mrs. Rodham was a wonderful, warm woman and when she passed, I really did miss her. One of my joys was taking care of her when she traveled with Mrs. Clinton. The president's stepfather, Mr. Kelly, was a salt of the earth rascal. He never failed to jump in the front seat when I picked him up from the airport because he didn't want to ride in the back seat and stare at my head while he was talking. A true southern gentleman.

And there I was, a thirty-year-old service man from Toledo, Ohio—by way of Arkansas—a part of it all. There is so much to tell of those times—too much to share in a single book and from a single perspective. Mentally, I have divided my memoir into four major sections. The first section tells of my ancestral lineage. The second section provides key accounts of my military and White House service. In the third section, my wife, Ronda, speaks from her heart about her upbringing, how we met, and how my service impacted our family, positively and negatively. In section four, former colleagues and friends talk about how we met and what stands out about our time together.

I'm grateful for each contribution from friends and colleagues, and value our varied perspectives of those times. Even so, I am well aware that we could never fully capture the essence of those cherished experiences. I can honestly say that the experiences have connected us in a way that few life events can. In the end, I feel both a responsibility and an honor to document and share my once in a lifetime appointment with history. In a sense, the end of our time together was a "last boarding call" for us all. We are each forever lifted and changed by it.

Part One

MY ROOTS

CHAPTER ONE |
A Gaelic Beginning

Gaelic Scotland—according to oral history documentation and census data—is where the Powell family roots... my roots began. My ancestors made stops in the West Indies before making their way to the Virginias and then Arkansas. Members of the family immigrated to the north, including Ohio in the twentieth century. The sir name of those earliest ancestors was "Brewer." They were what early ethnographers called the Alpine race, noted for their medium-light coloring, dark brown hair and shorter, broader stature. Archival records indicate that members of the Alpine clan fought for supremacy for three hundred years and inherited two islands on the west coast of Scotland. Apparently, they resided on these coastal islands for centuries before disbursing and migrating into Northern Ireland.

A Scottish uprising resulted in wider spread immigration, and apprentices and children were kidnapped and shipped to plantations. The American and Bristol ships transporting the kidnapped victims were classified under the name "Bolderston," and said to be part of William Penn's twenty-three ships.

Nicholas Brewer, Sr. was part of a family called the "Scarritt Clan in America." They were masons and adopted a secret name. Brewer and his family were one of the early settlers in the new world. They owned property and plantations in both North Carolina and Virginia. His first son, Nicholas Brewer, Jr., was born in North Carolina. In the late nineteenth century, the family took up residence in Arkansas.

CHAPTER TWO |
Mary Brewer of the West Indies

According to the emigration and passenger list of the early 1800s, Mary Brewer, formerly of the West Indies, was bound in servitude to slave master Nicholas Brewer in Louisiana in 1849. On board the slave ship, it is believed that a Rev. Dr. Peter Hastings and his wife, Jane from Ireland, succeeded in converting most of the passengers to Christianity. However, Mary had previously been baptized while living in the Scottish Covenant of Barbados, West Indies. Given their predicaments aboard those ships, like most slaves and indentured servants, the Brewers likely saw little reason to hope for freedom or a decent life where they were headed.

Upon arrival in the New World, Mary and other indentured servants and slaves were sent by Nicholas Brewer, Sr. to various colonies to work. Young Mary Brewer had learned to read and write while living in the Scottish Covenant. In fact, education and religion were highly respected in Barbados. There was practically no illiteracy in Barbados because so many people attended church and were required to both learn and read scriptures.

According to the 1850 Census, Mary Brewer, at twelve-years-old, was cited as a free inhabitant under the Brewer Township in Pulaski County, Arkansas. Mary must have gone through a culture shock upon finding herself in southeast Arkansas. Rather than the beautiful islands, the ocean and large bodies of pristine waters, there were endless acres of cotton fields, and forests, and the Arkansas River. As an indentured servant, Mary most likely cleaned, cooked, milked cows retrieved drinking water from wells, and performed other household tasks. The language and culture was a far cry from the

Barbados islands. However, the rice, corn, potatoes, and sugar cane she'd find in Arkansas would be somewhat similar to the sugar cane, Maize, yams and plantains of her early childhood on the islands.

Mary is believed to have spent most of her time inside the Brewer plantation home, unfamiliar with the slave housing concept. No doubt curious and troubled by Arkansan's slave society, she spent much of her free time interacting with the slaves during her chores of serving water to them. She spent hours filling the water barrels and driving the horse and wagon around the plantation to the work fields. Still a devout Catholic, she blessed the water before passing it to the workers.

A cousin, Lucinda, was worried that Mary was spending too much time with the field slaves. Lucinda suggested to the plantation owner's son, Nicholas (Nick) Brewer, Jr. that Mary needed more work to keep her mind occupied. As it turned out, Nick Brewer was fascinated by Mary and indulged her inquisitiveness. It is believed that Nicholas Brewer, Sr.'s family may have been involved in the abolition movement.

Plantation owners did not invite servants—Christian or otherwise—to their Sunday morning church services. Therefore, Mary joined the slaves on Sunday mornings at secret church meetings. Nick Brewer coerced a farmer by the name of Ben Thompson, who co-owned land with him in Rison, Arkansas, to build a church for the slaves. Nick Brewer donated four acres of land to build the church—Brewer Chapel—named after him. He appointed Mary as the head of the church. The Pope Piano Company, whose owner married into the Brewer clan, donated hymnal books and a piano to the church. The first pastors were Will Walker and a Reverend Booker. Mary led the first worship service, and some of the words to her first prayer were recorded:

Thank You, Lord, for this covered dwelling. Give strength, faith and hope to all who enter this temple to call upon Your Name, and seek Your will to be done.

24

Lord, help me to hand Your blessings down to my children and my children's children. Teach them that You are the way, that You hold the future now and forever. Amen.

CHAPTER THREE|
Mary Writes Arkansas History

Mary Brewer was a beautiful girl, dark complexioned with long, black hair and a slender build. In 1856, when she was eighteen-years-old, she gave birth to her first child, a girl she named Courtney. Her second child, also a girl, was named Array. It is said that Nick Brewer, who was twenty-five years older than Mary, was the father of both girls. Courtney and Array were baptized in Brewer Chapel.

Though her daughters were born "free," raising them was anything but easy. Courtney and Array were daughters of a servant, not daughters of the "master" of the house. Education was important to Mary, so she used the Bible to teach her daughters to read and write at an early age. They dressed well because Mary learned to sew in childhood, including altering dresses handed down to her.

Courtney Brewer was nine and Array was seven when slavery ended in 1865. An overjoyed Mary called the now freed slaves to the church to sing praises and give glory to God. The end of slavery, however, brought new challenges for the men and women who had never experienced freedom. Many families dispersed to other parts of the state and outside of the state to find jobs working as sharecroppers or farm laborers.

Mary, like some other indentured servants, received land to start their new lives. Therefore, she and her cousin, Lucinda, remained in the area. In those early days of freedom, the Brewer Chapel Church became an important institution for the black community. Courtney, Array, and their cousin, Anna Poplas (Lucinda's daughter) each sang in the choir. To wind down on Sunday evenings, the church members played baseball. They made bats out of tree limbs and balls from corn cobs stuffed with wool and cotton. The church chapel, which also served as a school by night, was located in the city of Pine Bluff. The girls traveled from Rison by horse and buggy each afternoon to school in Pine Bluff. Soon, the building was serving around the clock as both a church and a school.

Courtney and Array would both be married at Brewers Chapel and move to Pine Bluff with their husbands. Mary, who everyone soon began calling "Momma Mae," continued to lead the church. Her favorite song was, *We are Tossed and Driven*, which is believed to tell the story of God's promise, man's faith, and the travails of slavery.

According to census, both of Mary's daughters were mulatto. Array, for a time before she married, lived in New York, where she passed for a white woman. She attended school in New York and held jobs not traditionally held by blacks. When she married, she and her husband moved to Pine Bluff, where they owned a buggy, a café, a drug store, and a whisky store. She was well educated and had shares in a streetcar line. She had three sons who were well educated in New York, and later became a doctor, teacher and a minister.

Courtney and her husband, Anderson Powell, purchased twenty one acres of land from J.T. Porter Lumber Company in 1901. Nick Brewer had given Courtney a piano, a pair of cows and hogs as wedding gifts. The land was located outside Rison. When they realized they wouldn't be able to attend their church because of the distance, Anderson built his own church with the help of friends. Liberty Hill Baptist Church was named in honor of the Liberty Regiment, which was a black troop that fought in the Revolutionary War. Courtney and Anderson had thirteen children who were two years apart in ages. The first five children were born in Pine Bluff. All of the children attended school in Pine Bluff.

Many of Courtney and Anderson Powell's children eventually migrated to the north. One son, Thomas Powell, was married to Fannie Mae, and served in WWII. They had six children, including my mother, Margaret. Thomas Sr. was a third degree mason. Arkansas had masonic lodges throughout the state. It was common knowledge that the affiliation was helpful to blacks who sought employment.

Part Two

BLACK HISTORY IN OHIO

CHAPTER FOUR|
The Early Southern Migration

Ohio—as a requirement of the Northwest Ordinance of 1787—had outlawed slavery as early as 1803 during its first constitution. However, the state was hardly a utopia for blacks. Before Ohio became a state, very few blacks resided in Ohio country; only 337 lived in the area in 1800. Some were slaves, but most were free. The numbers of blacks in Ohio hovered near two percent of the state's total population throughout the first half of the nineteenth century.

In actuality, Ohio's proximity to Kentucky, which was a slave-holding state just across the waters, made Ohio a dangerous place for freedom-seeking slaves and former slaves. Before Ohio's statehood, many freed blacks who had left southern slave states in search of better living conditions, lived with Native American tribes. Although slavery was illegal in Ohio, slave owners still had the right under the United States Constitution to retrieve fugitive slaves. Many blacks hoped that slave owners would not look for them among the American Indians who lived in Ohio. During the late 1700s and the early 1800s, some black people settled in Upper Sandusky, a village of the Wyandot tribe.

While slavery was illegal in Ohio, some slave owners lived in southern Ohio. If a sheriff or some other law enforcement official accused an owner of violating the law, the slave owner would simply transport his slave or slaves across the Ohio River to the slave-holding state of Kentucky and force them to work there.

By 1810, approximately 1,890 blacks called Ohio home. That number almost quadrupled to 4,723 just a decade later. By 1860, there were 36,700 blacks residing in the state. Many of the new residents contributed significantly to the state's income and productivity, including their service in the "war factories" during World War I.

As cities such as Cleveland and Cincinnati began to grow many blacks moved there in search of better jobs and living conditions. Most had little money and could not afford to purchase land to become farmers, so they hoped to acquire jobs in the cities as factory workers or skilled artisans. The less fortunate among them took even lower paying jobs as day laborers, housekeepers, nannies, waiters, and waitresses.

Blacks moving from the south to the north quickly discovered that while in many instances jobs were far more prevalent and better paying, racism was as persistent in the north as it was in the south. They were relegated to one section of the city in substandard housing. Their neighborhoods, or "ghettos" as they were often referred to, furthered the continuation of the racial separation that was a part of Ohio's character and culture.

CHAPTER FIVE |
Ohio's Racial Conflicts and Civil Rights Struggles

Ohio experienced race riots during the early part of the nine-teenth century, especially in places where whites feared that blacks were gaining power or infringing upon opportunities previously reserved for them. In 1829, one such riot occurred in Cincinnati because Irish immigrants disliked economic competition from the black community. In 1830, Portsmouth white population forced approximately eighty blacks from the community.

Many chose to leave Ohio and moved to such settlements as Wilberforce in Canada. In those Canadian settlements, they did not have to worry about slave owners coming to claim them as fugitives. However, instead of leaving Ohio altogether, some formed their own towns in the state. Such was the case for Carthagena in Mercer County. During the 1840s, whites drove blacks from the area. Similar events occurred in the Scioto River Valley in the early 1800s.

After Ohio gained statehood in 1803, government officials enacted laws denying blacks their rights. At the Ohio constitutional convention, one vote denied black men the right to vote. During that time, women of all races were denied the right to vote. Edward Tiffin cast the deciding vote against the rights of free black men. Tiffin and his brother-in-law, Thomas Worthington, had owned slaves prior to moving to Ohio from Virginia. They freed their slaves, but many of those freed men and women followed their former owners to Ohio and continued to work for them as hired hands. Besides not being allowed to vote, black men could not serve in the militia or on juries. They could not testify in court against whites, receive assistance at the "poor house," or send their children to public school.

In 1804, the Ohio General Assembly, hoping to prevent any other black individuals and families from moving to the state, implemented an ordinance requiring them to post a bond of five hundred dollars to insure their good conduct. Despite the racism, many black Ohioans favored life in the state over being slaves in the south.

Fortunately, the American Civil War fought between 1861 and 1865 resulted in a Union victory. During the conflict, President Abraham Lincoln issued the Emancipation Proclamation, which freed slaves in rebel southern states on January 1, 1863. Lincoln issued this document as a war measure hoping that by freeing the slaves the south would have a more difficult time rebelling. While the Emancipation Proclamation did not free slaves everywhere, it was only a matter of time before the institution ended.

In 1865, the Thirteenth Amendment to the United States Constitution ended slavery. The Fourteenth Amendment granted equal protection under the law to blacks in 1867, and in 1870, the Fifteenth Amendment gave the men the right to vote. Most white Ohioans supported the Thirteenth Amendment, but passage of the Fourteenth and Fifteenth Amendments was difficult. The Ohio government actually approved the Fourteenth Amendment in 1867 and then revoked its approval in 1868. The Ohio legislature did not reauthorize approval of this amendment until 2003. The Fifteenth Amendment passed the Ohio legislature in 1870 by one vote in the Ohio Senate, and two votes in the Ohio House.

Ohio's black population soared during the first decades of the twentieth century. The Great Migration began in the 1910s and continued at least through World War II in the early 1940s. During this thirty-year period, hundreds of thousands of blacks moved from the south to the north. In the south, most of them had few rights and opportunities. They worked as sharecroppers, tenant farmers, or as day laborers. With the outbreak of World War II, numerous jobs opened for blacks in northern factories as white men enlisted in the United States military and went to Europe to fight.

While some black men also enlisted in the armed forces, many others moved north to fill recently vacated factory positions. Estimates vary, but perhaps as many as 500,000 black individuals and families moved from the south to the north during the 1910s and the early 1920s. Thousands who participated in the Great Migration settled in Ohio. They provided businesses in the state's industrial centers—including Akron, Cleveland, Toledo, and Youngstown among other cities—with eager, motivated workers. In 1920, blacks made up three percent of Ohio's population, but their numbers increased over the next decade to five percent of the population. The growing black population in Ohio altered the state.

Cities experienced a tremendous building boom during the 1910s and 1920s. For example, in a study of housing in Akron completed in 1939, it was determined that sixty percent of the city houses were constructed between 1914 and 1924, which is when the Great Migration was at its peak. Race riots started again in Ohio and other northern states, as some whites feared that they would lose jobs to the migrant minorities. Most blacks were forced to live in communities separate from whites. Despite the problems they faced in the north, the racism that they endured tended to be less overt than that of the south. The Great Migration did create new opportunities and hope for blacks who migrated northwards, but true equality did not result in the early 1900s.

Following World War II, numerous blacks and whites united to protest the racism and discrimination that existed in the United States. Beforehand, much smaller numbers of blacks and whites had fought for equality. However, as World War II concluded, a more organized effort called the Civil Rights Movement arose.

There were several reasons why the Civil Rights Movement developed when it did. A prominent reason is that hundreds of thousands of blacks served their country during World War II. They discovered that racial discrimination was not nearly as oppressive in European countries like Great Britain and France. Another primary reason for the growth of the Civil Rights Movement at the end of World War II was the G.I. Bill. To help veterans from World War II readjust to life after returning home, the federal government offset the cost of a college education. Thousands of black veterans sought to take full advantage of this benefit only to discover upon graduating from college that whites still received the better-paying jobs. Many blacks had to settle for jobs that they could have attained without a four-year college degree. Unhappy that the United States supposedly represented equality and freedom around the world, but did not truly provide such liberties to all, black individuals and their white supporters created a more organized movement to attain equality.

The Civil Rights Movement culminated in 1964 and 1965, with the federal government's passage of the Civil Rights Act of 1964 and the Voting Rights Act of 1965. These two federal laws outlawed segregation, guaranteed blacks equal protection under the law, and secured both the men and women the right to vote. While most people connected the Civil Rights Movement with the struggle to provide blacks living in the southern United States with equal opportunities, this reform era encompassed more. During the 1950s and 1960s, black individuals and families living in the northern portion of the United States also experienced racism and discrimination, although generally the racial obstacles they endured were not as oppressive as those in the south. Many black and white Ohioans actively sought to reform the south, joining organizations such as the Student Nonviolent Coordinating Committee and the Congress on Racial Equality, and participating in protests across the south, including the Freedom Summer Project of 1964.

Other northern activists also sought to end racism in the north, including in Ohio. For example, during the 1960s and

1970s, the United Freedom Movement sought to desegregate schools in Cleveland, Ohio. Partly due to pressure from Civil Rights activists, the Ohio government implemented the Ohio Civil Rights Act of 1959, which was to "prevent and eliminate the practice of discrimination in employment against persons because of their race, color, religion, national origin, or ancestry." It was to guarantee all people fair access to public facilities and private businesses. The Ohio Civil Rights Act established the Ohio Civil Rights Commission to enforce these stipulations, helping to eliminate discrimination in Ohio.

States such as Alabama seemed to have one of the largest contingents of black migrants to Ohio during the nineteenth century, but in fact, black men, women and even families came from every state in the south. Some of those families ended up in Toledo.

Part Three

THE POWELLS OF TOLEDO, OHIO

CHAPTER SIX |
Thomas and Fannie Mae Powell of Ohio

My mother was born in Toledo, though her parents migrated from Arkansas. My father was born in Atlanta, Georgia, though he too has roots in the deep south. Unlike most parents in my neighborhood, my parents did not work in the mills or car factories. My father, George Bowman, worked most of his life for Sears Department Stores, and my mother, Margaret Powell, worked for Kroger. Most families in our community were blue collar or middle class and lived pretty good lives thanks to jobs that they could get coming straight out of high school, following in the footsteps of their own parents.

Unlike ninety percent of the two-parent, married families in my neighborhood, my parents were never married. My mother fell in love with and had four children by a man who was considerably older. Except for the fact that my father never lived with us, he was not unlike other fathers I knew. I saw him literally every day. Looking back on it, I find it amazing that he never missed spending time with us on our birthdays or during important holidays.

My mother was born in 1936 to Fannie Mae and Thomas Powell, a prominent family in Toledo's black community. My grandfather, Thomas Powell, was one of thirteen children born to Courtney Powell who was the first daughter of Mary Brewer. My grandfather was born in Rison, Arkansas in 1892, attended school in Pine Bluff, and grew up working on his father's farm. He joined the military, and shortly thereafter shipped off to fight in World War II. Tom's wife, Fannie Mae, was a native of Toledo and an only child. Tom and Fannie Mae had six children: Georgia Mae, Thomas Jr., Mildred, Helen, Aaron, and my mother, Margaret.

Grandmother Fannie Mae was a no-nonsense woman. While she ran her home with what her children described as harsh discipline, she also shared a lot of love with her grandchildren, and we recognized and respected her role as matriarch of the family. She was the glue that held our family together.

Toledo's Numbers Culture

I sensed, even as a child that my grandfather, Tom, was unique in many ways. It would be years before I learned that he owned a pool hall and was prominent in the numbers running racket. Numbers running was rooted in the black community as an accepted part of the culture. In the numbers game, people bet on three random numbers and hope that those same three numbers are selected at random, the following day. The winner collects a certain sum of money. It is believed that Ohio was one of the origin cities for the numbers racket. All the big cities, however, had a numbers running culture. The Mafia did not get involved in numbers running until they saw how lucrative it was, and that was one of the main reasons they moved into Harlem.

There were well-known methods for coming up with numbers to play: The Red Devil, the Three Wise Men, and the Dream Book, which was an actual book of dreams that supposedly directed the reader to the winning numbers. People would dream about different things then look them up in the Dream Book to learn what numbers correlated with their dream. A few other numbers rules were that you never talked about your dream before 7:00 a.m. Also, whatever number you settled on, you had to play it for a week if you wanted to get lucky.

Many black communities also studied the "Blondie" cartoon, convinced that numbers were hidden in the cartoon illustrations. My wife, Ronda vividly recalls a childhood pastime of searching for the numbers hidden in the Blondie cartoon. Her mother would sit her down at the table and have her search until she came up with likely numbers. If there were two issues of the paper published daily, everyone believed that the late issue of the paper had the numbers in it. Numbers were purchased regularly at grocery stores and corner stores. Children were sent to the corner stores to purchase numbers for parents who were not able to do so. If your number came out, you would take your number slip to any store to collect your winnings.

It is believed that boxing magnate Don King served as a consultant for the state of Ohio on how to play the numbers. He had learned the system so well that people said the state eventually locked him out. The money became lucrative. Blacks ran the numbers before whites became involved and eventually gained control of it, although they said it was beneath them.

CHAPTER SEVEN |
Our Village on Fernwood Street

I was born June 8, 1962. My mother was twenty-six, and I was the last of her and my father's four children. Mother left her parent's home the year I was born. She moved into her own home just four blocks from my grandparents. Though she, my brother, my two sisters, and I no longer lived with my grandparents, all of our holidays were celebrated at their house. Their home remained the central place for the Powell family as long as my grandparents lived. My mother's siblings lived in Toledo, just blocks from my grandparents.

The Powell family was close-knit. I remember that my older brother Michael, who was around the age of twelve, asked if he could stay with my grandparents, and my mom and grandmother agreed that he could. My grandmother raised Michael as if he was her own child, and Michael would refer to her as "mama." He called our mother "Margaret."

One of my earliest childhood memories is of the Christmas holidays. My aunts, uncles and cousins came to my grandparent's home to enjoy the festivities. As the youngest of four siblings, my parents saw to it that I always got exactly what I asked for during Christmas. My siblings often would complain that I was my mother's favorite, and she would go out of her way to make sure I was happy. I was mother's youngest child, so a lot of that was to be expected. Even now, fifty-plus years later, I am still considered the "baby" of the family.

One of the things I will never live down is the fact that when mother started her career with Kroger Stores, she hired a nanny to take care of me. She later explained it was because she knew the job would demand a lot of her time, and she had to work to take care of us. Of course, my siblings saw this as another case of me receiving special treatment. How could I have known that I was probably the only black child in Toledo at the time whose mother had hired a nanny to take care of him? Her name was Ms. Sarah, and what I remember most is her cooking. She was an amazing cook. She remained a part of my life until I went to public school at the age of six.

Through her actions, our mother communicated much of what she would not say. She must have realized there would be obstacles to what she wanted to attain in her career. She knew she would have to work twice as hard to achieve her goals. At the same time, she didn't want to have to worry about my well-being as she went out and worked each day. In time, her hard work paid off, and she became the first black cashier and the first black manager Kroger Stores ever hired. She remained with the same company for over forty years before retiring.

Mother was a young teenager working in Derby soda shop when she met my father. I imagine theirs was a friendship that, in time, blossomed into love. My father was considerably older than my mother when they had their first child. My grandparents were livid, and tried everything in their power to keep their young daughter away from my father, even going to his business and threatening to kill him.

George Bowman was a well-respected businessman in the city of Toledo. He worked for Sears & Roebuck Company for most of his life, retiring in 1957. After retirement, he opened the Eureka Social Club, a popular members-only club in Toledo. In spite of the fact that he didn't live with us, I saw my father nearly every day. He was a loving and attentive man. My parent's four children were born three years apart. Our births were unplanned, so the three-year age differences remains a mystery.

My mother was much like grandmother Fannie Mae in that she was the center of her home. She was certainly a positive force in my life, the most important force, in fact. I can truthfully say that she taught me every good thing I learned in life…things that I was able to take with me throughout my life.

Beyond being a wonderful mother, however, Margaret Powell had a lot of ambition and devoted a great deal of her time to her job at Kroger. She believed in excellence and wouldn't stop until she excelled at everything she ever set her mind to accomplish. She expected the same of her children.

In her forty years as a Kroger employee, she worked at just about every store in the city. Her first job with Kroger was at the Cherry Street store. After that, she moved to the stores on Hauley Street, then Monroe and Detroit Street, Monroe and Central Street and finally on Monroe and Secor Road. In the early 60's, she became the first African American to work as a store manager. She always gave credit to her supervisor Robert Meegan who recognized her potential and mentored her at a time when blacks were rarely if ever hired in management roles. Margaret Powell spent every waking moment focused on excelling at work, and doing all she could to make life for her children better.

In return, she expected a lot from us. While she expected a lot from each of us, I believe she held her highest expectation of me. My siblings sometimes called me, the "Golden Child," of the Powell family, and I guess I always felt that I needed to try to live up to those expectations as well. Although I fought against the term when I was growing up, I now admit that I was a mama's boy who never wanted for anything that my mother wouldn't find a way to get for me. However, one thing she never gave me was permission to play sports. She was afraid I would get hurt.

While mother had been raised as a strict Christian and attended Calvary Baptist Church each Sunday with her family, no one would call her an overly religious woman. Attending church was not something she made us do on a regular basis. She taught the Christian rules in our home, but it was up to us whether we would continue to attend church after we moved from grandmother's home. Grandfather was a longtime member of the Masons and my grandmother was an Eastern Star.

My mother was a pragmatist. She understood that her work was important to holding our family together. I may have been a mama's boy, but Margaret Powell taught my siblings and me how to be independent and self-sufficient. We all learned to clean house, cook, do laundry, and sew. She knew that there was no way she could be a homemaker like my grandmother. My grandmother had my grandfather to serve as sole breadwinner. While our parents never married, and though my father was always in our lives, the fact that she was a single mother was a constant reminder to my mother that our well being, for all practical purposes, was her responsibility.

CHAPTER EIGHT |
Toledo's Seventies Experiences

I grew up during the sixties and seventies in the midst of the civil rights era. During those years, the civil rights struggle was at its apex, which meant racial conflicts were happening all around me. Amazingly, it wasn't until I left home that I was even aware of the struggle. Margaret Powell had sheltered her children from most of what was going on right in our own back yard. There must have been uprisings, sit-ins, maybe even riots taking place near our community...maybe even just blocks from us. I asked my siblings, and none of them can recall much of what was happening then either. I didn't realize all of what black Americans were going through, and I wouldn't learn most of my own history until I left Toledo, Ohio.

I think it boiled down to my mother having tunnel vision when it came to her family. She refused to bring anything inside her home that would negatively influence the way we saw ourselves or our sense of what we could do in life. All the while, she must have experienced racism and the backlash and tensions of the struggle first hand in the workplace. She never talked about racial prejudice or racism during all her years at Kroger. It would be many years later that she laughingly recalled a white customer at the store asking her, 'What makes you so special that you, a nigger, would have this job, over a hard-working white person?' Throughout my childhood, I don't recall her complaining about any of the obstacles she surely had to endure and overcome.

You would have to know Margaret Powell, my family, and my community to understand how we could grow up in the middle of some of the most pivotal civil rights struggles in Toledo—desegregation lawsuits, economic opportunity marches, and even a Black Panther office not far from our home—but not experience the negative realities of the struggle. Though we certainly weren't middle class, we were not poor and we didn't see ourselves as downtrodden. We were self-sufficient, and my parents made sure we never had to go outside our own home for anything. We weren't the only family who refused to paint ourselves as impoverished. Northern Toledo was a predominantly black, working class neighborhood in the sixties and seventies. Most of the fathers went to good-paying jobs every day, and most of the mothers were homemakers. In our neighborhoods there were some teachers, nurses and others who succeeded in factories. They worked hard, paid their bills, bought new cars when they needed them, and made sure their children had what they needed for school and for play.

I recall that my father was a no-nonsense type of man but good to the point that he would give you the shirt off his back. Like other fathers that I knew in our community, he was a great provider, a good role model and a family man. I also remember that he hated owing anyone and would always pay his bills with cash. It was common practice back then for most blacks to pay their bills off right away.

Not only was poverty not a regular topic of discussion in my home and immediate community, racism was something I had no experience with until much later in my life, and it wouldn't be in Toledo, but in the states of Arkansas and New York. My mother must have decided that we were better off not making racism and all of its tensions a part of our everyday lives. She was wise enough to know that we had to confront it someday.

We lived on the north side of Toledo, on Dorr Street, and in hindsight, our community was more like the "village" that you hear about nowadays—the village required to raise successful children. The families in our village knew each other, even most of the ones who didn't live on our street. There was very little crime as I recall. We looked out for each other. Our neighborhood was a thriving black metropolis. There were barbershops, corner stores, a theatre, and practically everything we needed. Unbelievably, I rarely saw whites during my childhood. If we saw them, we thought they must be lost or something was wrong.

I don't want to give the impression that we lived in village bliss because we didn't. Although I would be a grown man before I was aware of it, Toledo had a colorful side. We lived blocks from the "set," which was an area frequented by pimps and prostitutes. People played games of dice openly on the streets on a regular basis. Blocks away from our house, there was a window-less blue and gray building that I passed often—the local headquarters for the Black Panthers.

The Powell children, like all black children in the community, attended Lincoln Elementary, Robinson Junior High, or Scott High School in Toledo which were ninety-eight percent black. Even after the Toledo School Board agreed to have white students bussed to Scott High School, I don't recall it ever having a white student population over two percent. I enjoyed most of my high school years. I had some good friends, including my best friends, Terry Pritchett and Henry Brooks. We grew up in the same neighborhood, but Terry went to West Virginia to go to college, and I went off to the army. We remained friends throughout the years.

Monkey Hands and Twizzlers

When I was in high school, Kevin Taylor and Charles Phillips teased me about my long arms and big hands, and started calling me "Monkey Hands." That moniker has stuck throughout my life. My mother joined in the fun one Christmas by buying me a jacket that had "Glenn," across the front, and "Monkey Hands," across the back. Each Christmas holiday and birthday after that she would buy me toy monkeys. I embraced their teasing and the moniker. We have remained friends throughout the years. Sadly, Kevin passed away in June 2002.

Something else that stuck with me throughout my life that started in childhood is my near obsession with Twizzlers candy. I have no memory of how my fascination with Twizzlers began, but my mother indulged my obsession. She let me eat them every single day. When I left home for the army, my "Monkey Hands" moniker and my Twizzlers obsession went with me. When the army sent me to Hawaii, I immediately went searching the islands for Twizzlers. To my horror, they didn't sell Twizzlers in Hawaii. I wasted no time calling my mother and sharing with her the terrible situation that I found myself in—*Twizzlers-less*. As only a loving mother would, she went directly to the distributor warehouse that serviced my father's bar and bought boxes of Twizzlers at wholesale, threw in some monkeys, packaged them all up, and mailed them over to Hawaii *and* when I went to Germany.

Leaving School to Join the Workforce

I can't put a finger on what point, before joining the army, I decided school wasn't for me. I continued to go through the motions through the twelfth grade, but I left before graduating. I went to work for a local auto parts company by the name of Forest City Auto Parts, which I'd worked for as assistant manager during my high school years. It hadn't been too difficult to find a job back then.

Factories in Toledo like Champions Sparks Plug, General Mills, Hunt Foods, or one of the steel mills employed many of our parents. There were auto manufacturers nearby including Chevrolet, Chrysler, and Jeep. Libby Glass was a big employer back then, with its home office in Toledo. At one point, we were the glass capitol of the world for years. Standard Oil refineries were in the area. When young people graduated from high school many of them already knew they had a job waiting at one of the factories, mills, plants, or refineries where their fathers or mothers worked.

Chassis system railroads were big business in those days too. Goods in the country—subsidized by the government—traveled by train or truck. A student could graduate from high school one day and be making twenty dollars an hour working the next day. Of course, some young people did go off to college or, as I did, to the military.

Part Four

I'M IN THE ARMY NOW

CHAPTER NINE|
A Soldier's Story

Shortly after I turned eighteen, I enlisted in the army. Around that time, I learned that the young woman I'd been dating was pregnant, so going into the army would be an opportunity to provide for my child. The army sent me to Fort Dix in New Jersey for boot camp training on April 22, 1982. It was the perfect enlistment site for me. Fort Dix, New Jersey is where I completed basic training and advanced individual training as a motor vehicle operator, and remained in the area for a year.

The next duty station that the army sent me to was Fort Hood Texas. During that time, I took a trip home to Toledo and married my girlfriend and mother of my first child. I actually chose the assignment because of the popular television show, *Dallas*. I had it in my mind that I wanted to go to Texas and meet JR Ewing. Not only did I meet Larry Hagman, the actor who played JR, but I also met the entire cast at one of the big Dallas malls. That was in the eighties when the networks spent money to have cast members show up to greet their fans and when fans could easily get a photo with the stars. Meeting JR had been on my mental bucket list. Later, I learned that Klinger from *Mash*, and Danny Thomas were both from Toledo, and so I added them to the list.

In 1983, I was stationed in Hawaii as my next army stint. While there for eighteen months, I'm convinced that the Hawaii move helped me look long and hard at myself and my future. In Hawaii, I decided I needed to better myself. I enrolled at the Wahiawa Community School for Adults and got my high school diploma. My mother was so disappointed when I didn't graduate from high school, so I did it as much for her as for myself.

Also while stationed in Hawaii, I had a part-time job as a DJ at the NCO Club on stripper's night. It paid sixty dollars an hour, so I had extra money to send home to my son.

My long transportation management career began in Hawaii. A large number of applicants, myself included, had applied for a temporary mission of driving for the command sergeant major for the division. He was the senior enlisted man at the post. I beat out the other candidates for that position. Later, I drove for the one-star general on the post. After that, I returned to my unit and worked as the battalion mail clerk until I left in April 1985. While there, I met friends and mentors who would help me decide on my career journey. That same year, I was asked to re-enlist and First Sergeant Herbert Harris became a lifelong mentor and friend. First Sergeant Harris recommended that I choose Fort Eustis in Newport News, Virginia for my re-enlistment. I remained at Fort Eustis from April 1985 until January 1988.

I became squad leader and for the next six months, I managed a squad of truck drivers in and around the base. After that, I was set on transportation becoming my specialty, but my career trajectory changed some when I was appointed to head up NCO training, where I was responsible for the training of 270 soldiers.

Around this time, I met First Sergeant Fletcher Walker. He was sent in to straighten out our company and he did just that. He would stand up at the top of the stairs with his hat covering his eyes, but looking down at us. First Sergeant Walker was a 'soldier among soldiers,' an airborne paratrooper, a Vietnam veteran who had been shot three times. There was no one more surprised when he chose me to run the training. I knew he had high expectations, and I was determined not to disappoint him. He was the kind of leader for whom soldiers would fight and die. He was a true hero who taught me how to be a soldier and a man. He shared a lot about life with me. I imitated him in many ways so much that everyone would call me "Baby Walker." I met his family and it was an honor. He retired as a command sergeant major.

Part Five

A NEW CHAPTER IN LIFE

CHAPTER TEN |
Love and Marriage

A lot happened between 1985 and 1990. While still stationed in Hawaii, I realized that I was no longer in love with my then wife who had not come to Hawaii with me. Shortly after I returned to the states, while stationed at Fort Eustis, I began proceedings for a divorce. The divorce would be more problematic than I could have imagined. In spite of the fact that we had never really lived together as man and wife in the three years we were married, in the eyes of the law we were no less married.

The army shipped me to Germany in 1988, and I remained there for two years, working as squad leader of a heavy wheeled vehicle operator crew, driving tractor trailers and hauling mail. Spinelli Barracks was home for me then. Life changed during those two years in Germany for two main reasons. Sergeant First Class Sylvester Moore, who was the truck master, came to our company. He was very authoritative and we ended up having a run-in. He wasn't used to people not backing down. I didn't back down, and in the end, we became friends. He eventually told me he liked the fact that I stood up to him. He also inspired me in the way he handled himself. We forged a great relationship. I told him that the best mess hall in Mannheim was at Funari Barracks.

The second thing to happen—but the most important— was meeting a beautiful young woman name Ronda Holloway. One day, I pointed her out to Sergeant First Class Moore and told him I wanted to talk to her. I had no idea who she was, but found out later that she was from Cleveland, Ohio and had grown up just two hours away from me.

I watched her from afar for a long time. Eventually, I got up the nerve to track down a friend of hers and asked her—begged her—to give Ronda my phone number. A month passed and no phone call. I began following—stalking—her friend, pleading with her to convince Ronda to call me. Ronda finally called, and I asked her for a date. Ronda still reminds me that it was a lousy date and a lousy good night kiss. Our first date was at Burger King, so I understand why she thought that the date was lousy. However, there was a method to my madness. I figured that if she was good enough to eat with me at Burger King then she would be good enough to take to a fancy restaurant. I didn't want her to be with me just for my money.

When I told Sergeant First Class Moore about our first date, he predicted Ronda and I would get married. What happened was that Ronda and I fell in love, she got pregnant, I got shipped back to the states to one base, and she was sent to another one. Someone must have been looking out for us because Ronda's assignment got switched with a friend, which put her at Fort Dix, New Jersey, just three hours from Ft. Belvoir, Virginia. We were close, but three hours was still a long way away. After spending over four hundred dollars a month on phone calls and driving four hundred miles each week to visit her…plus nine dollars toll fares, I told her I was tired of going back to an empty barrack. It was by then clear that ours was a love that would last. Plus, our first son was already here and not adjusting well to the separation.

I took Ronda home to meet my family and while everybody liked her, there were a couple of glitches. My mother made it clear that we could not sleep together in her house while we were unmarried. We ended up spending the night at my sister's house. The second thing to happen was that when Ronda and I left my mother's house, she accidentally picked up my mother's keys to her new car. It was a while before we figured out that Ronda had the keys.

Part Six

THE GEORGE H. W. BUSH
ADMINISTRATION

CHAPTER ELEVEN |
Living the Dream

The saying goes that the big events in our lives come in threes: births, deaths, or even catastrophes. No one mentioned that sometimes the good and bad big things are jumbled together. My father died in March 1990, while I was stationed at Fort Belvoir. He died before he and Ronda had a chance to meet, which made his death doubly painful for me. I knew they would have hit it off. Because my father did not live in our home growing up like most of the fathers I saw in our community, the time we spent together was especially precious to me, and I think he felt the same way. When he was there, he was all there. He treasured our time together unlike some other fathers who may have taken time spent with their children for granted. I guess I took it for granted that he would always be there when I needed him. One of my biggest regrets was that I didn't get a chance to see my father when I came home from Germany.

The year after losing my father, Ronda Holloway became Ronda Powell. Our wedding took place in Alexandria, Virginia on May 30, 1991, at an attorney's office. Though it was a small, rushed wedding, it will always be the most important day in my life. Marrying Ronda was at the very top of my mental bucket list in 1991. Our marriage confirmed just how fortunate I was. I was twenty-eight-years old, moving steadily in my military career, had a wonderful circle of friends and amazing mentors, and a family who loved me unconditionally. Now, I was married to the woman of my dreams. I was beginning to think that maybe my siblings had been right all those years. Maybe I was that 'golden child' they had teased me about being. I was certainly living the American dream. I couldn't imagine my life being more amazing. How could it?

On Hold for the White House

The year Ronda and I married, I was working for the Army Intelligence and Security Command (INSCOM). I was the driver for a two-star general and took care of five other generals as well. I replaced Maurice Perry who left the job in a transfer to the White House to work in the White House Transportation Agency. It wasn't more than a year after he got there that Maurice called and told me there was an opening, and asked if I was interested in coming over to work. I told him I was and he said he would put in a good word for me with his boss, Sergeant Major Kamarmy. Not too long afterwards, I received a call for an interview. After the interview, I was placed on what is called "White House Hold" until my background check cleared. Although I already had a top secret military clearance, my White House clearance took four months. In September of 1991, I received my orders to report to the White House Transportation Agency. I had been officially cleared to report to work.

President George H.W. Bush was into his first term when I arrived. I remember how sad it was for his administration when he lost to President-Elect Bill Clinton in 1992. It took me a while to realize that I had a front row seat to witnessing some of the most documented events of our nation. It was an amazing realization.

To drive for the White House, I had to learn the lay of the land, which included D.C., Maryland, Virginia, and surrounding areas. Drivers training consisted of experienced drivers and me navigating the terrain. They would ask me questions about how to get to certain places. I could use a map, but of course learned that it would be best to commit these places and the area to memory as best as possible. The first time I met President Bush was in the motorcade. He walked over to another driver named Robert Gwyn and me and started talking. It was my first time being in the presence of the President of the United States of America. I couldn't believe it. The White House Transportation Agency was made up of mostly older military employees and a career civilian. There were just a few younger or new employees. After my drivers training was over, I began traveling with the press plane, doing logistics for the press office, the camera crews and the stenographers.

The Bush press office was a fun group. I met people like Marlin Fitzwater, who was press secretary for six years under Presidents Reagan and Bush I. However, Judy Smith, Special Assistant and Deputy Press Secretary, was my favorite person to meet in the Bush Administration. We would always eat potato chips together—*Utz* was her favorite brand. She would joke that she wished she hadn't stayed around until the end of the Bush Administration because people treat you differently when you call from the White House compared to afterwards. I'd come to the White House to drive the president's staff, yet I was fortunate to ride in Air Force One for the first time during the Bush Administration. After that first trip, I traveled overseas several times with the president.

The President and Mrs. Bush were friendly and treated their staff like family. Their dogs, Millie and Ranger, sat in the flight attendant's jump seats aboard the plane. This allowed the pets to see President Bush when he arrived on board. When the dates came around for Millie and Ranger's vet appointments, we would be reminded that the temperature inside the car had to be a certain level, and also that Millie and Ranger had specified seating arrangements that could not be changed.

One of the president's favorite vacation spots was Kennebunkport. I don't recall ever going there when they didn't eat at the famous *Lobster Pot*. One of the things that really amazed me during those trips was that all the vehicles were imported in— we had to call in advance to get cars into Kennebunkport.

Most surprising to me was the fact that President Bush would also import folks to play Horseshoes with him. He was a serious competitor and only wanted to play with people who would give him real competition. There was a handful of military aides or butlers who gave him good competitive games on a regular basis. Unfortunately, Horseshoes was not a game played much in my part of Toledo, so I missed my opportunity to compete against the president.

One of my most memorable moments of the Bush Administration was driving White House Advisor Fred McClure and the future Supreme Court Judge Clarence Thomas up to Capitol Hill to testify during the Anita Hill hearings. Fred McClure was advising Clarence Thomas before his testimony to Congress. Everyone knew about the Anita Hill case, and found it difficult to ignore the two men's riveting conversation. Fred McClure, at that time, was President Bush's only senior level black advisor. I was floored when I saw that he drove an old truck that he said belonged to his daddy. I recall that he left the Administration before it ended.

By far, the most memorable moment of the Bush Administration was election night, 1992. It was my first time on a campaign trail and probably the most painful one for everyone on Air Force One. I was working on the press plane that night and was a bit surprised to see the press' reaction to President Bush's loss. No one expected him to lose because his approval rating was at seventy percent. The plane ride back was eerie. You would have thought we were on our way to a funeral. My colleagues on Air Force One said the atmosphere was much worse. Reportedly, everyone on Air Force One cried on election night.

Part Seven

THE WILLIAM J. CLINTON ADMINISTRATION

CHAPTER TWELVE |
Arkansas Comes to Washington

The Clinton Administration came into the White House like a whirlwind. I had never before considered how significantly the culture of the White House changes with each new leader. It was evident that the Clinton White House would be quite different from its predecessor. The Clinton team tended to be *more* of everything—accessible, diverse, inclusive, and younger. It also seemed to leave itself open for more attacks. I worked especially hard to stay out of the way of the political conflicts that arose during those eight years. My role on the press plane made that difficult during the highly charged Travelgate scandal. At times like those, I was more than grateful to be *just* a military man.

During the Clinton Administration, I continued to work on the press plane. I became a part of the press operations for the last year and a half of the Bush Administration and the first two years of the Clinton Administration. I really had no complaints in either Administration. The people I worked with were great. The only thing I could possibly complain about was that once I started flying, I rarely saw my family. Yet, how could I complain when the same was true for everyone there? We got through those times by keeping a big picture in mind, and that was that we were working for the President of the United States of America and had jobs to do. That always put everything in perspective for me.

On the press plane, somehow I seemed to jibe with the reporters and news people. By far, the stenographers were my favorite group to work with. We always had a ball. As hard as my role in logistics was, we always found ways to get through those long plane trips from one state to another and across the globe. I became quite resourceful in keeping the press crew awake and myself entertained.

One of our favorite pastimes during the longer trips was a game called "SEATO." I actually learned the game from a Bush White House press officer named Sean. It worked great on the press office flights but would never have worked on the much more structured Air Force One. I enjoyed SEATO so much during the Bush years that I decided to carry it over to the Clinton press crew.

The game was most effective during our return trips when everyone could actually let their hair down and relax after completing their jobs. It was a way to fill the time between there—wherever *there* happened to be—and home. I would make my way to the intercom and make my announcement. "It's SEATO time...you can't win if you don't play." Everyone dozing or resting would immediately perk up. A pillowcase was passed among the passengers throughout the plane and stuffed with dollar bills with the press crew's seat numbers scribbled onto the bills. As this was happening, I would be humming the *Jeopardy* theme tune over the intercom to increase the suspense of the moment. The press passengers could play one, five, ten, and twenty dollars or any denomination they wished and any foreign currency they might have. The press plane's flight attendants played important roles in this game. They were the Vanna Whites of the White House press planes.

After everyone had put in their money, one of the flight attendants would pick a bill from the pillowcase and announce the seat number written on it over the intercom. The winner won the whole pot. There would be lots of excitement and joking back and forth. It was always a really exciting time, and we sometimes played several times if it was one of our longer flights.

Inside the White House, there were memorable meetings where you could feel the tension and the importance of the decisions being made there like the foreign affairs meetings at

Wye River, or the Camp David Peace Talks. President Clinton loved Camp David.

Understanding CARPET

I have never been shy about asking questions when I didn't understand something. One term—CARPET—baffled me for a while in those early days. The team of White House transportation employees I worked with early on were called the CARPET team for as long as I could remember. I tried figuring it out, but nothing made sense. Finally, I asked someone who had been around for more than thirty years. The CARPET team was distinguished from the non-CARPET team. At some point, White House operations decided they needed two different levels of cars for use by White House staff members. The difference was actually that some vehicles had carpet, and some did not. The president and his family's limousine, and all cars transporting special guests of the president and senior staff, must have carpet. All other cars used by lower level staff were uncarpeted. If you were brought to the White House as a CARPET driver, you would be driving for the president, his family, his special guests, and senior aides.

The White House itself is a remarkable place. I imagine when most people think of the White House, they think of that iconic photo that includes the south lawn, the west wing that houses the oval office and the president's immediate staff. There is so much more to it that most people don't get to see. There are the two conference rooms—the Cabinet Room and the Roosevelt Room—and a few tiny offices for top senior aides on the first and second floors. There is the East Wing, which, except for the East Wing oval office and a couple of other spaces, is pretty much the First Lady's domain. The East Wing is where some of the hardest work takes place. The State Dinners are prepared and presented there. The first family lives there. Special presidential announcements, programs, and visitors' tours all take place in the East Wing.

By far, the largest, and some would agree the most impressive building on the White House grounds is the Old Executive Office Building (OEOB), which was once the actual White House, but is now the site of the vice president's operations, as well as most of the policy and operational offices of the president. It is huge, stately, and possesses amazing architecture and history.

OEOB 89 ½ was the control center for my work during the time I worked on the press plane. Most people had no idea about this room because ninety percent of White House staff never traveled. The few that did, plus the press corps, all knew that in order to get your bags checked onto the plane, you had to deliver them to OEOB 89 ½ .

My name was synonymous with OEOB 89 ½. Ask the schedulers, the advance guys, the White House plane staff, the press corps, the White House press officers, and the president's medical or military unit. I was their go-to-guy for traveling stress-free anywhere in the world. I'm not bragging. I'm saying I took my job seriously. I recall distinctly one White House senior staff musing that their baggage would just "magically appear," whenever they arrived at their destination no matter where it was around the world. Magic had nothing to do with it. At the end of the day, I knew how important my role was in ensuring that the president and his staff got from point A, to point B without having to worry about losing one single item. Because of the temperaments of some of the people who traveled with the president, I can say that if my team did not get it right, we could get our heads delivered on a platter. My crew understood that our success relied on us first ensuring that each person delivered their luggage and personal items to OEOB 89 ½ when it needed to be there and not later so that it could be loaded onto the plane.

Secondly, we had to ensure that each piece of baggage was logged in and crosschecked so that when the travelers arrived at their destination, their baggage would already be in their rooms or would arrive shortly thereafter. If a staff person changed rooms or for some reason failed to board the plane at the last minute, we needed to redirect baggage so that they maintained connection with their belongings no matter where they ended up. So yes, OEOB 89 ½ was pretty much my domain.

Also stowed in OEOB 89 ½, was the unforgettable *Bertha*, which was the supply box for the White House stenographers. They traveled on the press plane as well. There were a couple of them who took turns traveling to ensure that all of the president's speeches or public announcements were documented for the press office, and for archival purposes. Just as its name implies, Bertha was humongous and took two people to carry on board. I would often joke with new press crew or passengers, "If you can carry Bertha, you can travel with us."

CHAPTER THIRTEEN |
Bound for Air Force One Glory

In June 1995, I was both excited and sad to leave the White House press plane, as I had been officially promoted to Air Force One logistics. One of the military aides, Rear Admiral June Ryan, introduced me to President Clinton and announced to him that I would be taking over Scott McQueenie's role as Air Force One logistics. The president asked me a few questions and said he was happy to have me join the crew. In time, nearly everyone who traveled with the president on a regular basis learned to trust my team. We were efficient and they regarded us as the professionals that we were. We worked hard to make sure everyone had a good experience aboard the plane.

Becoming a member of the Air Force One staff had its perks and prestige. However, the camaraderie I had enjoyed with the press plane didn't come so easily on the president's plane. I had to tone down my free-spirited, jovial ways quite a bit. No more SEATO! There was a new structure and less interaction between staff and crew, and for a good reason.

Air Force One was transporting the leader of the free world. He had the world's problems to contend with every day. If he wanted to do something fun, then we loved it. However, it was always his decision, not ours. Whatever the atmosphere, I realized without a doubt just how fortunate I was to be flying the world with the President of the United States of America.

Ronda complained that I didn't spend enough time at home. I took her complaints to heart. All I had to do was pull out my daily schedule to confirm that she was correct. She had every right to complain, though there was little if anything I could do about it, except find another job, and we both knew I wouldn't do that. Despite her disappointment about my being away so much, Ronda supported me. I can't count the number of times she had to rush out to meet me at Andrews Air Force Base with a change of clothes as I arrived from one country around the globe and was off to another. I usually had time to give her a quick kiss, tell her I missed her, ask about the boys if they weren't with her, and promise to call later. My schedule, like all White House staff, was determined by the president's schedule.

And, if anyone is interested, President Clinton's schedule was non-stop. He was documented as one of the most traveled presidents of the twentieth century. Here is a glimpse of what my day was like while working for him:

- Arrival Time: 5:00 a.m.
- Van Pick Up: 5:30 a.m.
- Arrival at OEOB, Room 89 ½: 6:00 a.m.
- Checking the manifest against each bag (domestic trip): 6:00-6:45 a.m.
- Load bags: 6:45-7:10 a.m.
- Depart for Andrews AFB
- Arrive at Andrews AFB DV Lounge to await for the Secret Service Technical Security Division (TSD)
- Once the bags were checked by TSD, proceed to the airplane for loading. (The airplane had to be loaded two hours prior to departure)
- Await the arrival of the first family on Marine One
- Off load any extra bags on Marine One, and put them on the plane. At this point, I would be the last one to board the plane.

The return schedule procedures were practically the same no matter what time of day we arrived. When I became a member of Air Force One logistics in 1995, it was campaign season. President Clinton did a lot of flying then. However, one of the most exciting trips he took wasn't a flight, but it was a train trip—the now famous train trip from Virginia to Chicago where the 1996 Democratic National Convention took place.

Mr. Clinton was only the second president in U.S. history to take such a lengthy campaign trip. One of his political heroes, President Truman, was the first. I witnessed firsthand that he seemed to enjoy every minute of that 1996 trip, including the thousands of voters who came out to the train stops and other places we set up for people to meet him. He was joined by historical figures like John Glenn and Rosa Parks. Senator Glenn even rode the train with him. During our Detroit stop, the president got to see one of his very first babysitters from Hope, Arkansas.

Two things are cemented in my mind about that trip. I met two of my heroes, John Glenn and Rosa Parks. But, I also had my first close up interaction with Mrs. Clinton. While I had interacted with Mrs. Clinton very briefly during the last four years, this was the first time I would interact with her for any length of time. After welcoming me to the team, she shared that she had concerns in the past about her bags being misplaced, or items being lost. She let me know how serious of a concern it was for her. Not only did I assure her that this would no longer be a problem, but I promised myself that we would never lose another item that belonged to the First Lady. From that day forward, I worked hard to make sure we didn't, and she knew it. She trusted me with her luggage and personal items.

That was confirmed when the Clinton family left the White House in 2001, and moved to Chappaqua, New York. Her assistant contacted me and asked if I would move her items from Washington, D.C. to her new home. I knew how important this project was, so I enjoined a few staff members I had great confidence in to help out. Traveling with me was James Ross and Mike Barker. To make a long story short, that move was one of those special projects that required all of my best instincts. In the end, the project was successful. The First Lady was pleased.

I was excited to return to New York for the opening of President Clinton's Harlem office. My crew Darryl Turner,

Doc Suarez, and JR were also present. We met at the famous Sylvia's Restaurant on 125th Street. We got to meet the singer Freddie Jackson and music mogul Russell Simmons who were both dining there.

I spent eight years with the Clinton Administration. There were great times, there were fun times, and there were times that weren't great at all. Without a doubt, altogether those were eight of the best years of my life. I met people that I never in a million years would have met had I not had the privilege of serving President Clinton.

The Clinton White House was filled with smart, hard-working people who, overall, believed in making the world better. I don't say that because I happen to be a Democrat. I say that because I am an observer of human beings. I talked, I asked questions, and I observed how they handled challenging times. Far more than the perks and prestige of traveling with the president, the people that I had the privilege of serving and working with side by side helped me to cherish those years like few others.

Everyone knew where the President and Mrs. Clinton stood on inclusion and diversity. The people who came to work for them either felt the same or set aside their real feelings. For example, before the Clinton Administration, the military staff could not attend White House events and parties. Only senior staff and managers were invited. I remember the day when White House aide Lorraine Voles went to President Clinton and asked why it was so. Just like that, years and years of restrictions were gone. It was the culture, and I was proud to be a part of it.

Those long sixteen and sometimes twenty-hour work days and long flights left a lot of time for reflecting on my life. I often thought about my life journey up to that point. Where I started out in Toledo, Ohio, was a long way from where I ended up… in Washington, D.C. working in presidential administrations… traveling with presidents of the United States. Even the worst or the most mundane events in life can prepare us for something greater if we endure…if we look long and hard enough for the lessons and commit to growing and learning from them.

International travel, as I stated, was one of the perks of my job, though it sometimes came with peril. The president's first trip to Moscow comes to mind. It is one of the longest foreign trips and one of my first. By the time we all arrived, I was starving but still had lots of prep work before we could eat. When we were finally able to eat around lunchtime, I ate two cheeseburgers. It wasn't one of my better decisions. By the time I got to my room, I was doubled over in pain, and shortly after came the nonstop diarrhea and vomiting. I called Ronda, all the way in Virginia, as if she could do anything from there. It was 3:00 a.m. her time, and she advised that I talk to the president's medical team. I felt foolish calling Ronda, only for her to tell me something I should have thought of myself.

I called Dr. Connie Mariano, the president's doctor who everyone was fond of and respectfully called Dr. Connie. After asking me a few questions about what I'd done and eaten since we'd arrived, she concluded that I had food poisoning. Members of the staff hauled me to the back of the plane, and Dr. Connie took care of me all the way home. She was wonderful. I decided later that there must have been a jinx on that trip. Labor Secretary Alexis Herman was also there. She fell on the ice and broke her wrist. I was never too excited to go on the president's trip to Moscow again. Of course I did, but from that point on, anytime I traveled Air Force One, Ronda prepared my meals to take with me. When my crew found out, they all asked for their own food bags. That terrible experience also taught me a valuable lesson. When I traveled overseas, the best way to dine was with the doctors and nurses, eating whatever they ate.

Food poisoning aside, there were some amazing incidents during those foreign trips, like the time one man's luggage traveled all over the country with us:

Luggage Gets Presidential Lift

Moscow – It's tough enough losing a bag on an international flight, but imagine the complications if your luggage ended up with the traveling party of the U.S. President. That's what happened to an Irish businessman who had the misfortune of sharing a hotel with President Clinton last week in St. Petersburg, Russia. The White House unwittingly scooped up the luggage of the man – whom Clinton aides declined to identify – and carried it with them to Moscow. Adding to the man's woes, his airline ticket to his next stop was in the bag. When the White House discovered the error, the bag was sent back to St. Petersburg at government expense, with a handwritten note from Clinton: "Sorry for the inconvenience. Your bags got a great tour of Moscow."

--Bill Nichols

As much as Ronda and I missed each other during those long trips, she later admitted that she enjoyed hearing about the trips and sort of having an inside look into the travels of the president and his staff. A time that comes to mind is when we'd just arrived at Greg Norman's place for the weekend, and the president took a bad step off a porch and broke his leg. No one could believe such a crazy accident could happen, but there it was. While the president eventually got to the place where he could joke about it, it certainly wasn't a laughing matter that night. He was in real pain and dishing out a few expletives. There was even an upside of that catastrophe. The president must have received over one hundred walking canes from all over the world. Some of them were stunning and made of some amazing materials.

The highlights of any soldiers' career are the dare-devil adventures. I don't think anyone told this, but I recall that once when we were flying in Alaska, Colonel Danny Barr was piloting, and for some reason, the plane was slowly sliding into the back-up Air Force One. Colonel Barr turned off the engine in the air and saved all of our lives. To have witnessed something that brought us all so close to death still gives me chills, but it also makes me proud to have witnessed Colonel Barr's piloting skills.

To encourage Air Force One passengers about how imperative it was that they be ready to leave when the president was ready to leave, we threatened them that if they were not where they were supposed to be—butts in the seats when the plane was ready to take off—they would be left. The only person the plane would make a return trip for was the president.

I can attest to the truthfulness of that statement because on one trip, the plane took off and left me. It was in Miami, Florida on a dreary rainy day. In fact, all the streets flooded that day. The president had gone to the golf course to get in a few games, but after the rain, he decided to leave early. I already had the plane loaded but had left on an errand with no idea the president would be leaving. When we traveled overseas, we had to be loaded three hours before departure just in case plans changed at the last minute. Though the president was making a stop in Jacksonville, Florida, I decided I would fly straight to D.C. so I'd be there when the plane arrived. A military truck met me at D.C. Reagan and took me to the Andrews Air Force Base to meet the plane. I was about an hour and thirty minutes early. When AF1 arrived, everyone was surprised to see me and relieved that I'd made it back. The military aides said everyone was looking for me and waited on the tarmac for as long as they could. This is how the White House press pool described that day:

Pool Report #4 - Trip of the President in Florida: Continuing the Fine Lockhart Tradition... October 4, 2000

The president decided to play golf on a rather soggy course this morning in Coral Gables. Your pooler missed the first tee and has nothing to report on whether Mr. Clinton wore waders. The motorcade from Biltmore to the airport was uneventful... except for the fact that the president finished his golf outing rather abruptly, hopped in his limo and took off while many of his staffers were not yet in their various vehicles. The incoming press secretary, who will not be named to spare him embarrassment, was left behind but managed to hop in a squad car. Glenn Powell missed the plane, sources said. Other aides, journalists and others were seen scrambling down the driveway toward rolling vans. Allow me to catch my breath. The flight to Jacksonville was uneventful. The motorcade left the airport slowly, allowing everyone to board their vehicles. Mr. Powell's whereabouts were uncertain at this hour...

Marc Lacey
The New York Times

Now I smile when I think back to that event. Back in those days, my colleagues would often ride me about my smile, how it was always there, how I always seemed upbeat and positive. I wasn't always upbeat and positive, but there was a whole lot to smile about...to be thankful for. I had a job that few Americans could claim ever having, and it hadn't been handed to me because they needed to fill a quota but because I'd proven myself as trustworthy and hardworking. I learned my job and could always do it better than anyone else. I'd been chosen for what I could bring to the job, and those skills and talents were deemed worthy enough for the President of the United States.

I admit that in the five years I worked on Air Force One, a handful of passengers tested my religion. I had to bite my tongue a few times to put it mildly. Once, a very well-known national leader mistook me for the bellman during one of our international trips, dropping his bags at my feet and giving me his room number. For the most part, the president's travel guests were magnanimous and respectful. I especially appreciated Governor Jay Rockefeller who I met during one of our international trips through the president's Deputy Chief of Staff Sylvia Matthews. It turned out that he didn't know the protocol for leaving luggage outside the hotel room on the night before departure. I made sure his bags were taken care of, and he thanked me profusely. When he asked if there was anything he could do for me, I jokingly told him to please consider writing me into his will.

There were a few "oops" moments that interrupted the normalcy of our travel and helped put some excitement in our long trips. On two occasions, the staff had to force themselves to keep a straight face when Congressman Gingrich and the Reverend Jesse Jackson—on separate trips—mistakenly headed for the front departure door of Air Force One, expecting to deplane with the president. One of the president's senior aides kindly told them that protocol required back door departures for all of the president's guests.

Out of all the foreign trips, I have fondest memories of Africa and China, the Taj Mahal, the Vatican City. I realized at the end of it all that I had visited six of the Seven Wonders of the World. As much as I enjoyed visiting China, it also turned out to be a logistics headache. Not the trip, but keeping staff's shopping in check. On that trip they could carry just one bag. Suffice it to say, Air Force One was never as loaded as it was during that trip.

There were other memories that will always stay with me from the Clinton Administration, like the day that a small plane hit the White House or the day that a man shot into the White House. We were just driving off the grounds onto Pennsylvania Avenue, when we heard a loud boom. There was also a second shooting, but both men were caught.

Part Eight

THE GEORGE W. BUSH
ADMINISTRATION

CHAPTER FOURTEEN|
A Decade of Service

My colleagues and I were emotional to say the least as the Clinton Administration came closer to its final days. The Clinton Administration established a culture unlike any previous president. Within that culture, everyone mattered and we felt that we mattered. We had grown accustomed to serving our country and feeling valued for that service. Staff members had become like family in many instances. It was not just direct coworkers that became like family but it was staff at every level from lower to senior aides. We had dined together in restaurants and eating joints around the nation and globally. Moreover, we had placed our feet in each other's homes and dined at each other's tables. We had formed genuine bonds, and it was hard to let all of that go.

As George Bush II arrived to the White House with his staff, I had mixed emotions about what was ahead. If the new president was anything like his father, he was going to be a super nice man. I wasn't so sure about the players who would surround him and work in the Administration. As expected, when the Clinton Administration was finally out and the Bush Administration was in, the culture of the White House shifted drastically. They had new ideas about the roles civilians, military, and political staff would play. Military staff was always ready for change. Change was our occupational norm. I learned that I would no longer work as Transportation Supervisor of Air Force One. Even so, I believed I had a role to play in the Bush Administration, and I did—Deputy Director of Customer Support and Organizational Development.

Maybe more than ever before in modern times, the steadiness of military staff would become evident as the tragedy of

September 11, 2001 was near. It stands out foremost in my mind concerning the time I served in the Bush II White House.

September 11, 2001

That day, I hadn't gone into work because I had orthopedic knee surgery scheduled, plus my family was in the process of moving. I'd misplaced my key to my storage locker and needed to go by the White House Credit Union for some money. As Ronda and I were driving from Quantico, where we were staying temporarily, we listened to the radio announcer describe the airplane hitting the Twin Towers in New York. We both began calling coworkers for additional information, but they did not know any more than we knew. Ronda and I began to talk about what if anything we could or needed to do. Just as we were trying to figure that out, the radio announcer reported that another plane had just hit the Pentagon. The plane crashed into the exact office location where Ronda used to work. We knew tons of people working at the Pentagon. We learned a little later that everyone made it out safely.

We knew we needed to go and pick up our sons. Traffic was at a standstill, and we ended up driving in reverse up an off-ramp in order to switch directions. We had what was then an off-brand telephone service called Cingular that we could freely use. Most people in the area were not able to place or receive calls because the phone networks were flooded. When we arrived at our boys' school, we had to show our ID before they would release our sons who also had to verbally identify Ronda and me as their parents. Other schools in the area and around the nation were on lockdown.

Pandemonium best described the White House that day. I was able to talk with colleagues who reported that they were in panic mode, mixed with utter disbelief. I remember thinking that day that if I had still been working logistics aboard Air Force One, I would have been with the president and not with my family. That day at least, I was delighted to have been reassigned from Air Force One to the White House Military Office.

CHAPTER FIFTEEN|
Second Chances

Second chances come in all forms at the most unexpected times in our lives, but they are worth their weight in gold. I've heard people talk about what they were doing on 9/11, how the tragedy impacted their lives, how it changed them for better or for worse. It was a wake-up call for Ronda and me too. Living through 9/11 together inspired us to give our family a fresh start.

It wasn't long after September 11, 2001 that Ronda and I started talking about the "R" word—retirement. Leaving work wasn't something I was remotely considering prior to 9/11—not so soon anyway. However, the events of 9/11 helped me realize how important my family was and how fortunate I was to have them. I began to think about conversations Ronda and I had had over the past nine years. Too many of our discussions were about me not spending enough time with her and the children. Ronda needed me. The children needed me. I needed them—I needed to be there. I wanted to make up for lost time if that was even possible. I had missed a lot as a husband and father, including birthdays, first steps, first words, and family events. I had even felt somewhat jealous when the boys would gravitate to Ronda and ask her advice about some of their problems instead of coming to me. But, what did I expect? She was the one who was there. I wanted to be there too.

I thought about the times when I wasn't sure things would work out for us. Ronda had been telling me for years that I was married to my job; the White House, the presidents, and first ladies were more important than my own family. I told her that it wasn't true, but I couldn't argue with how she felt.

Health Scare

The events of 9/11 had already begun to help me put my life in perspective. After much thought and talking with Ronda, I finally made the decision to retire from the army. My retirement ceremony was planned for January 22, 2002. An abundance of family, friends, and coworkers past and present would gather for my final goodbye. On that day, I was a proud husband, father, son, and brother. Most importantly, I stood as an even prouder soldier and American. I had given my country over twenty years of my life. After retirement, I would continue to work various jobs. I had been healthy while in the military. However, as you age, your body can start to break down.

One September day, Ronda and I were on our way to a local Steak & Shake for dinner. If I needed an extra nudge to help cement my rededication to my wife and children, I received it that day. I recall sneezing but holding it in. While we were at dinner, I began to feel a lot of pain. Ronda took me to the emergency room and the doctor told us that the force from holding in a sneeze had caused the pain. I had cracked a rib and bruised my chest muscles. All they could do was give me morphine. I had to heal on my own. That was the beginning. The cancer came later along with the realization that my life was not promised to me. The months of rehabilitation, physical therapy, and mental healing also came.

A Photo Journey

Early Life, Family, Friends

Glenn's birthday party, age three, with siblings Eileen, Mike, and Lauren (1965)

Grandparents, Tom and Fannie Mae Powell (Year unknown)

Mr. George W. Bowman, Glenn's father

School photo of Glenn, age five, (Lincoln Elementary, Toledo, OH) (1967)

Margaret Powell (Center), Glenn's mother, celebrating her
retirement with Glenn, Eileen, Lauren, and Mike
(Toledo, OH 1999)

Glenn and Ronda Powell attending the Air Force One Christmas
Party (December 1993)

Presidential Asia trip with coworkers John Henderson,
O'Neal Houck, Rudy Cunningham (1994)

Second Presidential West Africa Trip, Senegal, holding room for slaves (1999)

Glenn, Ronda, Darius, and Warren on Christmas vacation in Hawaii (December 2012)

Glenn's firstborn and nieces: (l to R) Tracey Odoms, Monique Ellis, Glenn W. Powell II, and Teshia Long

Glenn and Ronda celebrating Warren's eighteenth birthday in
Las Vegas, NV (June 2012)

Career Trajectory

M911 heavy equipment transport military vehicle (Fort Hood, Texas, 1983)

INSCOM driving staff: SGT Aldape, SPC Rice, PFC Kern, SGT Alvarez, and PFC Jones (1991)

Arrival ceremony for MG Kicklighter, incoming commanding
general, 25th Infantry Division, (Hawaii, 1984)

Departure ceremony for BG Runyon, Deputy Commander of INSCOM, (1990)

Birthday celebration aboard Air Force One (June 8, 1998)

Final reenlistment, White House Military Office with the
Honorable Joseph (Jake) J. Simmons IV (1999)

Trip site landing LAX, LTC Darryl Williams, Military Aide to the
President, with actor Chris Tucker, LCDR Vince Starks, Presidential
Nurse, (1999)

Air Force One Security Force, flight attendants, crew chiefs (2000)

Glenn Powell with White House senior staff aboard Air Force One
with The Honorable Tony Blinken, The Honorable Melanne
Verveer, and The Honorable Kelly Craighead (1997)

Glenn's retirement ceremony program

GEORGE BUSH

January 16, 2002

Dear Sergeant Powell,

Congratulations on your retirement from the United States Army after 20 years of service.

Our Nation owes a debt of gratitude to the men and women of our Armed Forces who risk their lives in defense of the freedoms we hold so dear. Throughout your career you have worn your uniform proudly; and as you leave the ranks of the United States Army, I join in saluting you for your dedicated service to country.

Best wishes to you in all that lies ahead. I hope your future proves to be as challenging and rewarding as your distinguished past.

Sincerely,

Sergeant First Class Glenn W. Powell
United States Army

OFFICIAL WHITE HOUSE PHOTO cGw0695 PR PJ4E934 -21A

SFC GLENN POWELL, U.S. ARMY
ABOARD THE 21ST CENTURY EXPRESS
AWARD CEREMONY FOR WWII VET.

CELEBRATING THE LIFE
OF
LEROY C. BORDEN

February 5, 1925 to March 16, 2007

White House Family and Other Dignitaries

President Clinton welcoming Glenn aboard Air Force One with
Rear Admiral June Ryan (June 1995)

Departure photo with President Clinton in the Oval Office after
final Radio Address (January 5, 2001)

Arrival photo with Clinton and Powell families (Detroit, MI August 15, 2000)

Glenn and Senator Clinton at Glenn's retirement ceremony, being presented the flag flown over the Capitol (January 2002)

Ronda and her mother, Gloria Banks, attending the final Clinton holiday reception (December 2000)

Glenn and his mother, Margaret Powell, attending the final Clinton holiday reception (December 2000)

Glenn with President Clinton, friends Jay and Doris Clark (Martha's Vineyard 1995)

Aboard Air Force One with President Clinton and Staff (August 1999)

Glenn and Kris Engskov aboard C-17 aircraft departing Bosnia (1999)

Glenn with President Clinton, O'Neal Houck, and Mike Ingram (Jackson Hole, WY, 1994)

Official retirement photo (January 2002)

Back stage at a fund raiser at the Warner Theater with President Clinton, Senator Clinton, Darryl Turner, and Dr. Gerald Suarez (2002)

Glenn with Chelsea Clinton during the hanging of the Clintons official photos in the White House East Room (2004)

Glenn with President Clinton, and James Stanfield (Martha's Vineyard 1993)

Glenn with Connie Chung (Haiti) (Date unknown)

Sylvia's Restaurant celebrating the opening of President Clinton's office in Harlem, NY, with Glenn, President Clinton, Dr. Gerald Suarez, James Ross, and Darryl Turner (2001)

To Glenn Powell
With best wishes,

To SFC Glenn Powell
With best wishes,

Bottom Photo: President Clinton, Senator John Glenn, and Glenn Powell

Part Nine

RONDA

CHAPTER SIXTEEN |
Growing Up in Cleveland

I was born in Glendale, Arizona in 1964, on Luke Air Force Base. My dad was in the Air Force. My parents divorced two years after I was born. My mother remarried in 1969, when I was four-years-old, and we moved to Cleveland where my stepfather's family lived. My mother, Gloria Banks, grew up in Phoenix, and my stepfather, Larry Banks, grew up in Georgia. My younger brother Marcus and I enjoyed life in Cleveland. He went to public school, but I went to a Catholic private school from third grade to high school—St. Benedicts Catholic School, and Regina High School, respectively. We were a blue-collar or working class family. Mother was a homemaker who never worked outside the home while she was married. My stepfather worked in the construction industry for state government. They divorced after thirteen years, but I always maintained a good relationship with my stepfather.

We lived in the inner city, which was on the east side of Cleveland. Ours was a predominantly black working class neighborhood, so economically everyone was pretty even. Unlike Glenn's household, my parents talked openly in our house about racism. The few white women who lived in our neighborhood were married to black men, so I never really experienced racial discrimination growing up.

I did experience prejudice from my own race because I was different from most girls in the neighborhood. I was a mama's girl, a daddy's girl, loved to read, and was a loner. Some girls prejudged that I was stuck up. I was more mature than the girls my age so I hung out with older girls, young women in their twenties, or my mother's friends. I felt more comfortable with them than I did with the girls my age. I was the neighborhood babysitter because I was the oldest girl on my end of the street, which meant I always had extra money.

I would say that my community was truly a village like Glenn's community. We certainly had that in common growing up. Parents knew the other parents' children and kept somewhat of an eye on us as we played. I didn't play outside much but I did sometimes. There were no electronic games and videos back then, so we used our imagination to create games, or we would read. At dusk, you could hear parents calling their children back home.

In our community, we had black-owned businesses as well as the standard businesses like Hudson's, and Samody's. There were black-owned restaurants and beauty salons, though I didn't go to a beauty salon until I was in the twelfth grade. Most black hair salons were operated out of private homes. There were also Jewish-owned, motels, hotels, clubs and grocery stores.

Growing up, I went through my tomboy phase but never grew out of my bookworm stage. I was content sitting at home doing my homework. I loved school, but it was a hard job actually getting to school. I had to ride a train and a bus to get there. I attended a predominantly white elementary school, then a predominantly white middle school, and then an all-girls high school. Talk about culture shocks.

As a young girl, I spent a lot of time in church by choice. My mother is Catholic and I am also Catholic. My father was Baptist. It wasn't until I got my first boyfriend in high school that I stopped attending church so much and started acting like a girly-girl. I dated the same boy off and on until he and I joined the military and went our separate ways.

I know Glenn talks about not enjoying school much, but I loved high school and was excited about the idea of attending college. I guess I knew already that my parents didn't have the money to send me. I remember asking my father to sign my loan papers so that I could attend college at Cleveland State University. He wouldn't sign the papers, but told me I should apply for work study. My mom filled out the papers without acknowledging that he lived with us. I received grants that paid for two semesters.

My mother was the disciplinarian in our family. My father was stern, but he raised us with tough love. He was a hard worker and he didn't believe in giving you anything—not even his children. He said we had to work for what we wanted. When he gave me money, he expected it back with interest. I remember asking my father for fifty dollars until I could cash my check. I needed the money to pay for something at school. He told me he would give it to me, but I would have to pay him back at fifty percent interest. I rarely asked him for anything. I started working when I was fourteen-years-old. Back then, you could work as a candy striper in the hospital. I was so excited, but when I went to apply, the starting age limit had changed to sixteen. Of course, I was disappointed but I was not giving up.

My mother and I had stopped at Church's Chicken to have lunch and I asked the manager if he was hiring. He asked how old I was and I told him fourteen. He said that if I could start right now, I had a job, since he was short-handed. Well, my mother left me there and I got to work. The manager forged the age on my paperwork to reflect sixteen.

Mom was a submissive wife in the traditional sense of the word. My dad would dole out an allowance to her for paying the bills. At a very early age I realized I didn't want that kind of relationship with a man. Although my mother stayed home, I grew up around many women who worked outside the home. I made it up in my mind that I would be independent and not depend on a man.

I grew up wanting to become a flight attendant or an airline flight ticket agent, or a candy striper at a hospital. Back then, you could become a candy striper at fourteen. I never imagined myself getting married even though I knew I wanted kids. There was a neighbor who worked with foster kids and did cook outs for them. Those kids really touched my heart.

Once my grant money for college ran out, I went to work fulltime to help my mother out and to have spare money. I worked at Uncle Bill's. It was something like Walmart. When it closed, I went to work at Zayer's, working at the jewelry store. They closed, and I was out of work for six months until I got a job with Giant Eagle Grocery Store as a cashier/office assistant. All the time I was working, I never owned a car and would use public transportation if I needed to. If I worked late, my mother would meet me at the bus stop.

My parent's divorce was around 1983, after I'd graduated from high school. My mother took it hard. She had been completely dependent on my father and had never really worked outside the home. Now, she had to. She got a job as a school crossing guard in the neighborhood, and worked at that job for several years. She eventually took a job as a housekeeper with a hotel. She worked there for thirty years until she retired. We used to joke that I became my mother's "husband," helping her take care of my brother.

CHAPTER SEVENTEEN |
I'm in the Army Too

From about 1982 until 1987, I worked to help take care of our family. Then in 1987, I decided I needed my own place. That same year, my brother started to show interest in the army. Sibling rivalry was all too real in our home. We bet each other twenty dollars that we could outscore the other on the admission test. I scored higher, and when it came time for us to enroll, he changed his mind. My mother was not happy at all that I was enlisting in the army, but she understood. It wasn't that I wanted to be in the military as much as I just didn't want to become a statistic in Cleveland like so many other girls I knew.

I enlisted in June of 1987, and was scheduled to leave November 17, 1987. The career field that I chose was personnel specialist. I was depressed knowing I had to go home and mentally prepare my mother for my departure. The night before I was scheduled to leave, the recruiter gave me the option of spending the night in a hotel or at home. I opted to stay at home but made the mistake of going out and partying, so the next morning I changed my mind about going into the army. However, I decided I should keep my word and left the following morning to start my new journey. My mother was so distraught she couldn't think straight at work that day. It was ironic because the Federal Building was right next to the hotel where she worked. We actually went in at the same time. We said our final goodbye on the street. She went her way and I went mine. The pain in my heart was unimaginable and I know that she felt the same way. This was the first time that we had ever been apart. While I was inside getting my travel items and instructions together, my mother kept looking out the window for me, and when she saw me walk out with my suitcase, she just about fell apart. It was as if I was leaving her life forever.

I was shipped to Fort Jackson, South Carolina, but was able to come home for Christmas. When I went back to Fort Jackson, I was there until February of 1988, and then I returned home again. I volunteered to go to Germany for two years, and left in April of 1988. My mother was at work when I left, but when I got to the airport I couldn't get on the plane. I believe my nerves had gotten the best of me. Since I couldn't talk to my mother, I did the next best thing and called her best friend who was like a mother to me. She told me to take a drink and I would be okay. I did, and boarded the plane.

I didn't like Germany or being so far from home at first. What I did like was German food. I loved currywurst – a sausage made with curry; German ham hocks, and jagerschnitzel - basic pork chops with gravy and mushrooms. I also loved their Black Forest Cakes, which was the most popular dessert there. German-style Chinese food was quite different from what I'd had in the states. It was much fresher.

I was amazed to see that the Germans dressed up to go to the grocery store the way we dressed up to go to a nightclub. They had what they called "long Saturdays," which is the first Saturday of the month, when the grocery and other shops stayed open until 5:00 p.m., rather than closing at 2:00 p.m. It also took me a while to get familiar with some of the cultural differences. At that time, as a general rule, women didn't regularly use perfume or deodorant.

I started out working in personnel in 1988, which is where I remained throughout my military career. Working in personnel, you see every soldier's personnel record. When Glenn first asked me out, I already knew he was divorced and had a child, although I was waiting for him to tell me. Speaking of our first date...I was not impressed to say the least. Glenn arrived wearing sweat pants, British Knight tennis shoes and a Members Only jacket. We ate at Burger King. I thought he was cute and all, but his brotherly kiss left me doubtful about a second date. I admit by the second date, it had gotten a little better. Our second date was at a nice German restaurant but way out in the woods. I thought, 'is this man' about to kidnap me...?' We ate weiner schnitzel and French fries. Our romance continued to blossom.

When we married in May 1991, Glenn was twenty-eight and I was twenty-six. We got married in Old Town Alexandria in a lawyer's office. I remember it was hot and Glenn was having second thoughts. He walked me around the block twice before we actually went into the lawyer's office. We spent our honeymoon at his barracks and had Churches Chicken for our wedding day meal. The next day we would travel to Ohio to attend his sister's wedding. I had to do a twelve-month stint before I left Fort Dix in New Jersey to establish a household with Glenn. It so happened I had already completed my twelve-months.

After our wedding, I moved from New Jersey to Maryland, where we established our home together as man and wife. I went to work at the Fort Myers Transition Point in Virginia and worked there for a year. After that, I went to work for the Secretary of the Army, in the Personnel Service Center from 1993 until 1997. Afterwards, Colonel Jake Simmons hired me as his administrative assistant at the White House Communications Agency. Everyone who has ever worked at the White House will tell you that the first day is little scary. You recognize that you are in a rare opportunity surrounded by amazing people making history. You also feel the weight of it from the moment you walk inside, and you don't want to mess it up.

I worked as Colonel Simmons' administrative assistant in the headquarters office for three years. After that, I asked if I could return to personnel. I worked in different areas of personnel so I would keep learning and add to my toolbox. I received several promotions in my twenty years of service. It's been a joy, but also a challenge. Because of Glenn's job, I didn't always have the spousal support I needed. I am fortunate that my bosses became my work-village, supporting me in so many ways. They allowed me to reschedule my work hours, loaned me a computer and allowed me to do homework at work when I decided to go back to school. I was also blessed with great babysitters who kept our boys all night if I had to go out of town, go to class, and prepare for tests. I absolutely loved my work.

Before I retired, they asked me to work with civilian personnel. There was no manual in place to tell me how to do it, so I asked them to train me. I would go to training three times per week. In October 2007, I went to work for the White House Communications Agency as a civilian, working as the civilian personnel manager.

CHAPTER EIGHTEEN|
New Beginnings

When will it be my time? That's what I found myself asking my mother on some of our phone calls during those days when Glenn was away on his job. My mom is still my best friend, and I trust her. She promised me that my time would come once the kids were grown up and out of high school. She was right. I retired from the military in November 2007, the same year Darius, our middle son, graduated from high school. I remember he'd asked me if he could get a tattoo when he graduated from high school, and I told him when he graduated, not only would I pay for it but that I would get a tattoo with him. The day after he graduated, we went together and got one. That was June 2007.

Glenn retired in 2002, and that's when he and I began to reconnect as a couple. Part of it might just be that we're getting older together, but hopefully it's also that we're getting wiser too. What I do know with absolute certainty is that it is very rare for dual military couples to last. It is pretty normal for military people to marry multiple times. Neither one of us wanted to be one of those statistics. I can't even explain why we stuck it out, because there were certainly times I think we both wanted to give up and call it quits. There was something that made me hang in there. This was Glenn's second marriage, but I wanted it to be my only marriage.

Our relationship has been interesting, hurtful, full of surprises, more than I would have ever imagined. Today, we're stronger in our love for each other. Getting older and wiser has helped. There's even more for us to explore with each other. Glenn had suggested that we celebrate our marriage at twenty years. If we do it, it will be beautiful, but huge and exhausting. I think what saved me and my mental health was when I left and went to school for three months. We had a terrible fight before I left, and I think that was my way of crying out because I felt I was losing myself. He felt as if I was abandoning them, but I was finally doing what I needed to do for me. I was happy those three months, not having to worry about taking care of anyone but me. Glenn was so angry...Warren was less than one-year-old. The second time I went off to school, it was easier for all of us. Glenn was retired. Finally, I think our children began seeing our relationship as it should be. That wasn't the case when we were both working for the president.

When I find myself feeling bitter about how we almost lost our relationship, I remember what was instilled in both of us in the military, and it's that our lives revolved around God and country. I guess I never thought that kind of commitment might actually ruin my marriage and family life. I've seen it happen too often. I can truthfully say that after my retirement, we fell deeper in love. We found out that we like to be together.

Glenn has talked a lot about how some of the best things in our lives came out of some pretty horrific things. Well that, is exactly the case with Glenn's illnesses. Neither one of us could see it coming. Glenn was one of those people who was rarely sick, and if he was sick, he ignored the symptoms and kept going.

When we first learned Glenn was sick, we were at the doctor's office and Glenn didn't hear the full story that the doctor was telling him. All Glenn heard was the word, "cancer," not the part where he said, it may not be cancer. He was absolutely devastated, and I found myself having to be the strong person for him and for the kids.

Glenn was terrified of cancer and death. Not only did he totally shut down, he totally shut me out. When I would ask him what was wrong, he would say nothing was wrong and I knew it was a lie. In time, my concern changed to anger. Soon, I pretended like I didn't care and wasn't concerned either. If he didn't want my help I wasn't going to beg him to take it. His worry and lack of communication started to turn into depression. It got to the point that he needed therapy. When we went to the first therapy session, I asked if he wanted me to go with him. I thought I was just going to support him, but it turned out to be a group therapy session. Finally, he was dropping his guard and letting other people in. I wanted in as well. I had for a long time. However, the therapist gave me a reality check. She told me that the more I fussed at Glenn, the more he was going to shut down. It was a defense mechanism. I had to stop trying to force my way in and try a gentler approach. I was fussing because I was terrified of losing him. From that point, we went to two more therapy sessions before his scheduled surgery, and Glenn finally began to feel better, which gave me a lot of relief. I had been feeling as if I was losing my best friend and that he had given up on me and our family.

Once we got over that hurdle we were met by one crisis after another. With each crisis things got better. He didn't want to go through surgery, but I told him I wasn't ready to let him go yet. In large part, because we went through all of this we began spending more time together. Sometimes I think maybe it's too much time together. We still need our individuality and space to be ourselves. Glenn doesn't really want to spend much time with anyone else now.

Our children are Glenn Warren Powell II, who is thirty-four (Glenn had him when he was eighteen-years-old); Darius, our firstborn is twenty-seven; and our baby, Warren, is twenty-two. Glenn lives in Toledo, Ohio and Darius and Warren live at home and attend school. Darius and Warren are close to their father but remember the times when he was seldom around. They weren't really aware of what his job entailed but knew he worked at the White House and with the president. He took them on tours of the White House a number of times, and they met his colleagues. They both saw me as the strict disciplinary figure when they were growing up. Their dad was usually trying to make up for not being around that much.

Part Ten

AN ORAL BIOGRAPHY OF GLENN POWELL FROM WHITE HOUSE MILITARY COLLEAGUES, CHILDHOOD FRIENDS, AND PRESIDENTIAL APPOINTEES

Mike Barker, former employee, White House Transportation Agency

I grew up in Dennison, Ohio, and joined the army when I was twenty-four-years-old. I was a motor transportation operator in the military. I went to the White House Transportation Agency in 1999.

I met Glenn a couple of months after arriving at the White House. He chose me as one of his traveling crew. My first perception of Glenn was that he was personable and had great work ethics. He got along well with his crew, and everyone had a lot of respect for him. It was an honor to be a part of his team. We worked in a pretty much "no error" situation every time we traveled. I traveled on AF1 all over the world. I remember once in Moscow I had jumped from advance mode to fly back with Glenn's crew. Once we were about to leave Moscow, I realized I didn't have a Moscow Visa. That was scary. I had to get to the airport and through the Russian Security Service. We were all in a sedan together when a security officer stopped and asked if I was secret service; everyone hurriedly said "yes."

One of the fondest memories of our time together was the last day of the Clinton Administration. Glenn, James Ross and I were at President Clinton's house helping him move his stuff from the White House to their new home. It meant the world to me that Glenn chose me to be a part of their team.

Reginald Barnwell, former White House Colleague

I live in Woodbridge, VA with my wife, Jacquie, who I met while in high school in Miami, FL. We spent some time stationed in Panama City, FL and then transferred to the Pentagon where I worked in the Secretary of Defense's Correspondence office, and Jacquie worked at the Bank of America, Pentagon branch office.

I met Glenn at the Pentagon. We would see each other in passing and strike up conversations. To me, Glenn is like a brother from another mother! The man is a leader with integrity and a tremendous amount of self-initiative. Glenn pushed himself at work like few people I ever saw. However, he's a man with strong family bonds. He is there for them.

When Glenn retired, he began to pull his circle of friends and family even tighter. Once you're his friend, you will always be his friend. He enjoys a bit of suspense too. When Glenn takes us to dinner, we can never know where we're going until we get there. Besides that he never lets anyone smoke in his car.

I have good memories of our time together in the White House, but one stands out. *Jet* magazine came to do a story on the number of African Americans working in high levels in the Clinton Administration. Well, somehow Glenn ended up in that picture. We all laughed and said that Glenn was a black Forrest Gump.

Bobby Batts, former Operations Supervisor, White House Military Office

Glenn is a professional and caring human being. We met when I arrived at the White House in 1996, and our friendship has continued since then. I only recently retired from the White House in March 2015, and accepted a position at the State Department as a General Service Officer. Back in the day, Glenn contributed a great deal of mentoring in my life to help get me through the early days of working-in-the-White House overwhelm. I followed his example of professionalism on the press plane and then aboard AF1.

From our first encounter, I could tell that Glenn was a take-charge guy. I also noticed that he always walked around with a bag of Twizzlers candy in his pocket, which he never shared. It shocked me when I learned that Glenn couldn't play any sports... not ping pong or pool. He didn't even play dominoes. For all of those shortcomings—if you can call them that—what meant the most to me about Glenn is that you could count on him being direct. He says what he means, and he means what he says.

Terry Bell, former White House Transportation Agency Senior Resource Manager

I began working in the White House Transportation Agency in 1999 as a sergeant first class and received a promotion to master sergeant while there. My first job was a human resource specialist, which entailed logging the travel, finance updates, and all other actions that dealt with office records. At that time, there were eighty-eight soldiers on the White House Transportation staff. One day, this gentleman with such a humble demeanor walked to my desk. The man was Glenn Powell. Being infantry in my early days of the military, I was not accustomed to that kind of humility from the soldiers that I had worked with in the past. From that first encounter, I knew he was a class act.

Eventually I became the agency's physical fitness test trainer. I contacted Glenn because it was time for the annual physical fitness test. Because he traveled so often, he was not able to take the scheduled fitness test. I would have to work around his schedule. When he was informed that it was time to take the test, he called me up and said, "I hear we need to take a test at 0500 *a.m.* in the *morning*." He didn't like physical fitness training or working out, but he was always out front before anyone else.

Mr. Leroy Borden, who was the White House director of transportation, had been there for over thirty years. He gave Glenn the nickname "Zero Error" because he was the epitome of excellence and work ethic. Mr. Borden stated that Glenn would do anything and everything within his power to accomplish his mission. He never showed anything in his countenance except that he was happy to be there. He set the bar extremely high for other soldiers.

In all the years that I have known him, I have never observed Glenn Powell abuse or misuse anyone, and for that, I would describe him as amazing human being. No matter how far he advanced, he reached back to help others. Glenn took time from his busy schedule to give my mom, son and wife a White House VIP tour. He also made it possible for me to meet and interact with the then First Lady, Hillary Clinton. I had the opportunity to take a picture with her, which is framed and hung in my living room to this day!

With Glenn being in such an important position, he provided not only me but other soldiers with special White House and AF1 tours that we could not have experienced otherwise. I can safely say that those days are over for most soldiers who work in the White House now, but thanks to Glenn he helped make memories for my family that I will be able to tell my grandkids about. It is an absolute pleasure to be his friend!

Earnest Caldwell, Retired Army Sergeant, White House Transportation Agency

I am a retired army sergeant and I spent eleven years at the White House. Like Glenn, I worked for three presidents. I served as a driver and chauffeur and also traveled with the presidents. I was assigned to James A. Baker III, as a driver and am still working for him. There was another White House driver from Andalusia, Alabama, and the other drivers joked that the White House probably hired the only two people from Andalusia. The other person was Retired Master Sergeant J. D. Blue. I retired from the White House in June 1993, just as Glenn was getting started there. After retiring, I ended up staying in Washington and continued working for Mr. James A. Baker III.

I first met Glenn in 1991, through my supervisor, Mr. Leroy Borden. I didn't know Glenn well, but I learned more about him after I left. Mr. Borden was manager of the White House Transportation Department and was the person who brought Glenn and me together. He was an amazing man and leader, and saw early on that Glenn had a lot of potential.

We learned that Mr. Borden was dying sometime in 2005, and agreed that we wanted to go and pay our respects. His doctor approved it, and all of his former employees from around the country traveled to Alexandria, Virginia to say goodbye, and thank Mr. Borden for all he'd done for us over the years. That was something to see.

It was after Mr. Borden's death that we decided to start the White House Alumni Group, and invite the military staff, everyone who worked in White House CARPET/ Transportation, on AF1, and the press plane. I was the president of the group, and Glenn was the vice president. Glenn is a great commander and connector. We worked closely together to make sure the White House Alumni Group was a success. We had some amazing times, cookouts, dinner on the river, Christmas parties, etc. Glenn was always so energetic and that much energy in one person can be annoying. However, I will tell you what wasn't annoying. Glenn was task-oriented, and he always got the job done. He never just took a person's word for anything, but always verified it for himself. He had a way of getting through walls and barricades on the job that we didn't even know existed.

Pam Carpenter, White House Stenographer

Whoever appointed Glenn to his position at the White House was a genius. I don't exactly recall how we met, but considering Glenn's personality and professionalism, he likely walked to our office, located in the Old Executive Office Building and introduced himself. I began working at the White House Stenographer's Office in 1984, during President Ronald Reagan's second term, continuing service under Presidents George H.W. Bush, William J. Clinton, and George W. Bush.

Once Glenn took charge of transportation logistics, he traveled and worked closely with the stenographers' office. One of his responsibilities was to coordinate logistics for the press plane when we traveled and he did this impeccably, always making sure we had what we needed to perform our official reporting and transcription duties. One of Glenn's most-used phrases was "piece of cake" when he was working. Everything was a piece of cake no matter how sticky or precarious the situation. His confidence in himself, and his abilities, and years of training kept him from becoming rattled, often in some extremely trying situations.

Glenn is a family man, always focused on his wife and children. His exemplary attitude and wisdom have served him well in life. I know that's mostly his upbringing, but I also think part of it is his military discipline. Without question, Glenn is a rock solid individual. If you're caught in a raging battle, he is the guy you want in the foxhole with you. I truly cherished his friendship during those years of working together, and I am proud to say our friendship continued long after we both left our positions at the White House.

Rudy Cunningham, former employee White House Transportation Agency

I was born in Waterloo, South Carolina. I joined the military in 1976, and remained there until 1979. I received an honorable discharge after two years in Fort Hood, Texas. I came back to South Carolina, and was there between 1981 and 1984. I went to Fort Bragg, stationed in Panama from 1984 to 1988 and returned to Fort Hood from 1988 to 1990. I got married in Germany in 1981, and was there until 1992. In 1992, I was assigned to the Pentagon for six months and served at the White House from 1992 until 1998.

Glenn took me under his wings when I arrived at the White House. He would come over to the Pentagon and talk with me. I trained for work on the press plane, and for six weeks, Glenn and I traveled together. Even when we were tired, we found a way to have fun. When I started driving, Glenn convinced Mr. Borden to let me work with him. When Glenn transferred to AF1, I remained with the press plane. We would both travel during the campaign season.

Few people knew that Glenn was afraid of flying. When we'd travel with the press plane, our crew would always be seated toward the back. Well, Glenn would usually be the first on and would create this tent and completely cover himself up. We wouldn't see him again until we arrived at our destination. I don't remember Glenn getting up to eat or use the bathroom. However, once we arrived, he'd pop up all refreshed. Although he didn't like to fly, I don't recall him ever getting sick on a flight. There was that one time he got food poisoning in Russia and had to fly back on AF1. We were all trying to help him, and he was so sick he couldn't put his pants on. It wasn't funny then, but later on we all enjoyed ragging him about that. Glenn's wife, Ronda, and I worked together at the Pentagon. They are both good people, like family.

Jeff Elder, former White House AF1 Flight Attendant

I was born in Niagara Falls, New York, and worked on AF1 from 1991 until 2006 as a flight attendant. Working as a flight attendant is stressful. Working as a flight attendant aboard AF1 is especially demanding. We had to make sure that everyone enjoyed his or her flight, and Glenn was especially good at it. I think a few people resented Glenn because he worked so closely to the president. However, Glenn is the type of person anyone would want working close by, the president included.

Glenn and I hit it off because we have similar personalities. He is a people-person, fun, outgoing, and trustworthy. I recall a flight to California when we met the actor, Chris Tucker, who had a great time laughing it up with the flight crew and taking pictures. We enjoyed picture-taking, and Glenn took a very memorable picture on the last flight of President Clinton's. That was the flight where the crew was majority African American. I don't think it ever happened again.

Our work relationship grew into a great friendship, so much so that I invited Glenn and his wife to my wedding. Unfortunately, they were not able to attend due to one of their sons being ill. I remember that

Ronda always introduced herself as "Glenn's wife." She clearly had a lot of pride in him. Knowing this, I would always mess with him calling her my baby. I gave Ronda a picture of me during her retirement party. She hung it up on her wall at work.

One of the things I remember best is our discussions about the red hot water bottle that hung up in our bathrooms at home while growing up. We would laugh to the point of tears talking about it. This was in the beginning when we started working on the plane. When I retired, we were still making jokes about those hot water bottles. Glenn framed a hot water bottle and gave it to me as a retirement gift.

Glenn has the ability to relate to people on all levels. What you see is what you get, and I think most people respond well to Glenn because he is comfortable in his own skin. In addition to being a family man, Glenn is a real mama's boy! He talked a lot about his mother on those flights.

Noy Garner, Military Colleague and close friend

Glenn and I met at Fort Eustis where I was the training NCO, and he was one of my assistants. He was a "64 Charlie" military truck driver and always our designated driver when the guys had a night out. He taught us about the trucking side of the transportation business, and when we served together at Ft. Eustis, he insisted we all learn to drive different types of equipment.

I remember working with Glenn on assignment assisting a marine unit on its way to Camp LeJeune. We deployed to Camp LeJeune to discharge cargo—

mostly cars and trucks—onto vessels taking equipment overseas. Glenn was shorter than everyone else, but he had these huge hands and he more than carried his own weight that day. At some point, I learned that when he was a boy, people used to call him "Monkey Hands," which he used to the fullest advantage. Even at his retirement party years later, he was jabbing the secret service with those huge hands! He had a tremendous work ethic and a dry wit about him. As fate would have it, I was the Security NCO in charge of clearing Glenn for his first job in the White House.

He enjoyed travel and looking for new adventures. Glenn, a bunch of friends and I used to run around together in Hawaii and back in Arkansas (Texarkana). Once, a bunch of us got together to go to a local barbershop in Texarkana. This young man was cutting my hair and all of a sudden, the clippers turned off, and the lights went out... no electricity! This woman yells over at the young barber, 'I told you not to cut them boys' hair.' I think I left the shop with half of my hair cut! We had some amazing times back then.

After we all started retiring from the military, Glenn became the glue that held us all together. Few of us would have kept up with each other the way we did had it not been for him. Glenn is a dependable, loyal person, but if I had to select only one word to describe him, it would be lovable. I am a twenty-two year military man, and outside of my family, he is one of the few guys who I would say 'I love you' to, and it wasn't just words. I know, one day he called me and said he needed a deck built onto his house. I threw my stuff in my truck and spent the next few days there building his deck. He would do anything for people, and people would do anything for him. I think he had that kind of effect on almost everyone who met him.

D. Stephen Goodin, former Presidential Aide to President William J. Clinton

I grew up in Texas, went off to college, and ended up interested in politics. I did advance work beginning in New Hampshire for the Clinton campaign, and when he won, I joined the transition advance group. Of course, there weren't a lot of big trips to advance during the transition, but I did get to meet Clinton aides Bruce Lindsey and Nancy Hernreich. I ended up going to work at the DNC for a couple of years. In 1994, when Andrew Friendly got burned out in his job as President Clinton's personal aide, Oval Operations Director Nancy Hernreich asked if I was interested. I was, and came over in October of that year.

One of the important components of serving as the president's personal aide is keeping up with the many documents and items the president received during public events at the White House and during domestic and international travel. That included his clothing, books, his crossword puzzles, his official gifts from a sick child, etc. Glenn, at that time was part of CARPET, and was a huge help to me in securing and keeping up with everything.

In the middle of a global flight, on many occasions, the president would ask for something just as I am falling asleep. I would have to get Glenn to take me down to the pressurized belly of AF1 where all the president's bags were stowed. Glenn would always have this smile on his face and would take me right to the place I needed to go. Glenn never seemed jaded or fed up. I never saw him give me the eye-roll. He was just doing his job and was proud to be there to do it. While a lot of us start out that way, it is a challenge to hold on to that kind of fresh perspective in the White House jobs despite the immense honor of being there. I sensed that there was real joyfulness in Glenn. Now, he might tell me that he was faking it, but I would be surprised by that. I never sensed that he wasn't genuine. I don't imagine he was happy every moment of his life, but his smile would just light up the world.

Many times when I was absolutely frantic about something, Glenn's smile would be so reassuring. He was so reliable and focused. He was solution-oriented too, and the least likely person to pitch histrionics when there was a problem. Not only did he hold on to the honor of serving, but he always did it with infectious joy.

O'Neal Houck, former White House Transportation Agency Supervisor for Reagan, Bush, and Clinton Administrations

I grew up in Sumter, South Carolina, and my family was sharecroppers and farmers. I joked with Glenn that I grew up very different from how he grew up, in Toledo, Ohio. I was one of eight children in our household, and our father, now in his nineties, was an extremely hardworking man. I spent twenty-two years in the military. In 1987, during the Reagan Administration, the White House hired me. I worked under presidents Reagan, Bush, and Clinton, and met Glenn in 1992 when he came on board toward the end of the Bush I Administration. Glenn started out in our section, and I took him under my wing.

The only thing I had over Glenn was experience. He was far more charismatic. I recall that he was ambitious, upbeat, and a stickler for perfection, always doing everything to the best of his ability. Glenn knew a little bit about everything and he knew everybody. He really is an extraordinarily good guy. He likes to be around serious-minded people, but he also likes to have fun. He works at connecting and keeping people connected. Glenn is what I describe as a half-and-half-man, meaning he is both a good businessman and a good family man.

Glenn does so many things well that one of my funniest memories of him is when he didn't! When he first started his training at the White House, he was backing the car up and hit the wall. Unfortunately, the boss was sitting right there at the time.

Bob Lehman, former employee White House Transportation Agency Shift Supervisor and Dispatcher

The best way to describe Glenn is dependable. I was one of the shift supervisors when Glenn assumed his responsibilities in support of AF1. There were twenty-seven of us at the time. He took special pride in his work, and was willing to do whatever he needed to do to get his job done. He didn't require any special treatment. He just blended right in.

In my role, I supported Glenn in what he needed as far as transportation requirements, ensuring that he could get things back to the White House, including all the press pool equipment and luggage associated with the trip. Glenn made the work very easy to do as he was always precise in what he needed. During the years that we worked together, Glenn was a total team player and always wanted to get things done in the most efficient manner. I retired before he did. Since so many of us have retired, Glenn has assumed the role of pulling everyone together every year. He is definitely a family man who values relationships.

Rear Admiral Dr. Connie Mariano, Retired Presidential Physician and Director of the White House Medical Unit

I was born in the Philippines. My father was a U.S. navy steward. My mother was a dentist. We moved to Pearl Harbor Navy Housing Project when I was about two years old. I grew up as a Navy brat and entered the military in 1977, through the military medical school in Bethesda, Maryland.

I arrived at the Bush I White House in 1992, and remained through the early first term of Bush II. As far as remembering when Glenn and I met...it's almost as if Glenn was always there, though I probably met him during one of the president's trips. Glenn worked with Ninja-like stealth. He was part of the smoother machinery of the White House. He was always in the background, but it was also common for him to go up to the second floor—the first family's residence—which most workers didn't do.

We traveled together internationally a great deal, and it was extremely stressful. Coordinating luggage belonging to the presidential traveling party is so very important, but somehow Glenn made it appear seamless. In our down time on those trips, we would go and eat with Glenn. We all wanted to hang out with him. We had to work the streets many times on trips, and Glenn had street smarts. When we'd discuss people who were traveling with us, Glenn was always a great judge of character, but you'd never find him badmouthing anyone.

I recall when Lou Merletti, Director of Secret Service, retired that we did a really funny video. In the video, Glenn did a monologue about Lou Merletti's hair products. If you know Lou, his well-groomed hair was pretty well known. It was hilarious.

I know that the White House could be a rough environment with lots of adversity from time to time. I have experienced being underestimated by peers or supervisors. You just learn to deal with it and know that if you keep doing what you're supposed to do, some good will come out of it. I believe Glenn shared the same philosophy about adversity and life. Glenn always exhibited great confidence and integrity that I think may have been borne out of tough times. I really think Glenn should run for office!

Wayne McLean, former employee White House Transportation Agency

I was born in Laurinburg North Carolina, and I grew up in a farming community where my mom worked in a textile mill. My grandparents worked for farmers—my grandmother doing domestic work and my grandfather working as a farmhand. I've been married for thirty years and have one child. My wife is from Americus, Georgia.

I joined the military and retired as a master sergeant. I worked for Homeland Security and served during three Presidential Administrations. I also worked at the White House from 1996 until 2005. I was part of the famous White House CARPET (Transportation) department, and it was one of the best experiences of my life.

I met Glenn in January or February 1988, in Manheim, Germany in the driving academy where we learned the rules and regulations for driving in Germany. He drove a tractor trailer. My first impression was that Glenn was a funny young man but one who could be very serious when he needed to be. He already had a good idea of what paths he wanted to take in life.

Glenn had a different outlook than most of us guys. He wanted to go to school and better himself, and so did I. Glenn and I had a class together where the instructor did a lecture. After the instructor left, Glenn got up and gave us his version of what the instructor had said but also about us improving our lives, getting our education, bettering our lives. That made an impact on a lot of young soldiers.

Maurice Perry, former employee White House Transportation Agency

I was born in Lancaster, South Carolina, and raised in the town of Kershaw. I graduated from Andrew Jackson High School 1979, and decided to the join the army because there were only factories in my hometown, and I wanted a different career. Four weeks after I got out of high school, I was on my way to Fort Dix New Jersey for basic training and AIT. My job skill training lasted from June until August 1979.

My first duty station was Fort Lewis in Washington State. I was there from August 1979 until August 1982. In August, 1982, I transferred to Arlington Hall Station in Arlington, VA with duty at the Pentagon in Washington. I worked as the chauffer for the deputy chief of staff for intelligence.

In 1983, I transferred to Heidelberg, Germany for four years, returning to the United States in May 1987. I was re-assigned to Arlington Hall Station in Virginia, working at the Pentagon as the chauffer for the chief of staff of intelligence. It was during that time, I met Walter Sherrod who worked at the White House Transportation Agency and he became my mentor.

Beginning in 1990, Glenn and my career pretty much shadowed each other's. When he returned from Germany in 1990, he was assigned to my old duty assignment working at Fort Belvior, VA for the chief of staff of intelligence. He worked there a year before joining me at the White House Transportation Department. This occurred during the Bush Administration, while I was working on the White House press plane. Glenn and I both ended up working together on Air Force One. I recall that Glenn got sick on the press plane and the president's doctor cared for him, so they put him on Air Force One. I joked that he was trying to take my seat on Air Force One.

After retiring from the White House Transportation Agency in 1999, I joined the United States Secret Service and worked there for twelve years. I retired from the Secret Service in 2012, after having a major stroke in 2010.

Glenn had a great personality and was a dedicated family man who was education-minded. He always wanted to learn as much as he could. He was the kind of guy who always took the ball and ran with it. He was all about the job and the mission first. Most important, he was about family.

Tony Powell, former White House colleague, and close friend
I am originally from Jamaica. I came to the United States in 1970, and lived in New York City (Bronx). I joined the navy in 1977, with no idea that it would become a career. I served in the United States Navy for twenty-eight years, including seven years in the White House. I retired at the rank of master chief (e-9) in 2004.

I met Glenn in 1997, when I was command master chief and deputy director for Presidential Food Service at the White House. Glenn worked in logistics for Mr. Clinton's travel. Glenn and I traveled together quite often. In fact, one day, General Colin Powell, Captain Elliot Powell, Glenn Powell and I ended up in the west wing lobby of the White House at the same time—four Powell men, all unrelated.

My first impression of Glenn was that he was a caring person. If you ever needed help, he was there. Although our career and branch of service was different, we met at the White House for one purpose, which was to service the commander-in-chief. We believe we provided the best service to the president and the first family.

Glenn and I interfaced a lot when he worked for President and Mrs. Clinton. He always worked to discover a solution to just about any problem we encountered. If we weren't traveling together, Glenn would locate me and give me the lay of the land, especially when plans changed. I knew he was in my corner, and he hasn't changed. He is the same today as he was back then.

I can sum up Glenn Powell as a true patriot and an outstanding professional. When we all began to retire, Glenn is the one who worked to keep us connected. He helped to organize the White House Transportation alumni reunions, and he always made sure I was invited.

Joseph Ramseur, MSG, Retired, Army, Career Counselor

I was born in Trenton, New Jersey and I grew up in Greensboro, North Carolina. My mother died when I was three-years-old, which is how I ended up with my father's family in Greensboro. Two years after graduating from college, I joined the military to help take care of my family.

The first time I met Glenn was in 1985, in Fort Eustis. What I remember most is that he had a brand new car that year, which was exceptional for a young guy that age. It was an Audi, and it got a lot of young soldiers' attention. At the time, Glenn worked in the motor pool, and I worked in the headquarters. Glenn always tried to associate with positive people. He worked hard to make the most of his skills set. As a natural organizer, he loved bringing people together.

I know Glenn to be a straight shooter. He's not a "yes" man. If he sees something that needs to be addressed, he will address it. By and large, Glenn is a family man. He and Ronda have been together for as long as I have known him. Though he was committed to his job, he was also committed to his family. Ronda has helped to keep Glenn balanced in life.

Sonya Ross, former member or White House Press Corps.

My bureau chief assigned me to the White House on September 11, 1995. In my early thirties then, I was young by black journalist's standards. I showed up doing race and civil rights before the White House noticed how white the environment was. Working there as a black journalist, I stuck out like a sore thumb. When I took POTUS (President of the United States) trips, it was a comfort to be around other black people. I remember seeing Glenn marching around like he was in charge of everything. He was friendly, and overall, AF1 seemed to be more integrated with black crew and stewardesses. I traveled an awful lot. I was one of five people rotating in pairs. If the president took one hundred trips a year, I took about fifty of them with him. In 1996, it seemed like I was on the plane an awful a lot. I traveled with Hillary Clinton to Scranton, Pennsylvania, and then to Latin America. Glenn was to me the shining star on the foreign trips.

Around 1997, we were on an African trip with Hillary, and went to Tanzania. She had the better safari. We pitched a tent and had lunch on the Serengeti. We would get there and there would be "shop opps" where the local crafts people would come out and sell their wares. There was an American woman married to an African, selling a wrought iron lamp, a standing lamp with a ceramic body, and a black linen shade. Her husband had made it and he was able to find a matching standing vase. I asked about the price of the lamp. She said she had a problem selling it because of the universal plug. It was a teardrop lamp. We haggled a little bit and came up with thirty-eight dollars. Thanks to Glenn, it traveled from Africa back to the states unscratched. I picked it up with my baggage. However, I managed to break the vase—my outrageously good African bargain—when I got home. The lamp is still with me, and I'm so grateful to Glenn. He looked out for us like family. I didn't want to exploit his generosity. Everybody went shopping. Most people would have refused but not Glenn. I remember seeing Glenn during the start of the Bush years but I don't remember seeing him after that.

Glenn, in one word, is "Brotherific!" He has a solid, black guy vibe. He is culturally, intellectually, politically, professionally, and socially straight out of the black experience. You pick up on it. He has a universal charm that endears him to you. I always knew I could rely on him to have that certain brother cultural understanding of where we were going and what food we should eat. On the Hillary trip to Africa, when we were doing the "shop opp" in Cape Town, they ultimately had to limit people to two cases of South African wine. I had bought five cases of wine. Everyone had bought numerous cases of wine and were weighing down the plane. Luckily, when I went back with Colin Powell in 2002, they had free shipping. They were kind to accommodate our wine.

During those days, I recall that Glenn was so convivial. It's like you didn't even have to ask for his help. I saw him unflappable in times of intensity. He was a military man to the core, but relatable. I never saw him tense. He stayed calm, making things run efficiently. He had natural leadership composure. On those trips, I never saw him moody or with a pickle face. That suggested to me that he had a happy life outside his work. I strived to be that kind of person to separate work from private life. I could tell he could.

Walter Sherrod, former employee White House Transportation Agency Logistics Supervisor
I was born in Columbia, Mississippi, and I spent twenty-two years in the military. Twelve-and-a-half of those years were in the White House. I arrived in April 1988, assigned to the USATA (WH) Transportation Agency as a chauffeur. After five years, I went on night shift and was promoted to supervisor. In 1998, after ten years at the White House and being out of military mode, I went to Korea for a year. Afterward, I was assigned NCO Academy. Two years later, I returned to the White House in 2000, and was there for two years—the last year of the Clinton Administration, and the first year of the Bush II Administration. After retiring, I worked for a company near

Capitol Hill for three years. I eventually moved to Florida in 2005, and loved the weather.

Glenn and I had been in some of the same military circles, but hadn't really met until we were both working at the White House on the same shift. I was promoted to supervisor of that shift shortly after Glenn came on. The White House can be a difficult place for employees to develop close friendships. However, when Glenn came on, I thought that he had the kind of personality that made forming a friendship more natural and more likely.

The thing I remember was that Glenn was responsible and resourceful. He was very detailed during presidential travel, particularly with instructions and assignments, and he was resourceful in helping get toys donated to our transportation agency's' holiday parties, and recruiting officials to attend. The USATA (WH) annual parties collected the most toys, had the most participants, and impacted more children during the years Glenn participated.

At Glenn's retirement luncheon, it was amazing to see the number of people who returned, most of whom we hadn't seen or heard from in years. Everyone remembered how Glenn loved his Twizzlers. He would not play with you if you messed with his Twizzlers. He carried them on every trip.

As energetic as Glenn was, he had no athletic skills. None. He would sometimes come to our pickup games and watch us play. However, he was a team player in every sense of the word, especially when it came to our job and mission. Glenn is loyal. Once you are part of his circle you always are.

A.T. Smith, White House Secret Service, First Lady Detail Leader

I transferred from the Miami Secret Service Field Office in 1994, after eight years there, and joined the president's protective detail. In 1995, I was briefly assigned to the First Lady, before returning to the president for the 1996 re-election campaign, and continued in that role through the 1997 Inauguration. After the inauguration, in 1997, I returned to Mrs. Clinton's detail as lead agent, and remained in that role until 2000. Most of Mrs. Clinton's travel during that time involved promoting women's issues, with special focus on micro-lending for women around the world. As lead agent for her secret service detail, I traveled to more than eighty countries, including pre-advance trips that I had to do before her travel. Her popularity had grown, and that meant her level of security increased.

Glenn was already at the White House when I arrived in 1994. Given his proximity to the first couple, we saw each other fairly regularly. What I noticed about Glenn was how outgoing and gregarious he was. Over time, we developed a friendship, and I realized that he is everything anyone would want in a friend—always there when you need him. Glenn and I interacted all the time after that.

One indication of Glenn's "can do," attitude, was the fact that well before I returned to Mrs. Clinton's detail, she asked Glenn to assist in trouble shooting a problem that had become persistent. At the time, Mrs. Clinton and her staff relied on the host embassies to provide strategic support, but for whatever reason, that arrangement wasn't working. The result was the loss of a bunch of her luggage. It became a logistical nightmare, especially on the military plane on which she mostly traveled. After Glenn moved over to work with her, the White House military office began to do more, and Glenn began to coordinate logistics for the First Lady's travels. Ken Haskins also came on board to help in that coordination. Thanks to Glenn and Ken, Mrs. Clinton would not lose one bag in the next three years. Glenn Powell is, without a doubt, a "can do," kind of guy.

After I left the presidential detail, I was transferred to the Secret Service headquarters, then later to the Office of Human Resources and Training. While I was assistant director of human resources and training, we hired Glenn to serve as quartermaster in charge of all supplies and logistics at the James J. Rowley Training Center. This gave me an opportunity to see Glenn's work close up. He did a great job, and brought a positive, professional approach to every task.

Dr. Gerald Suarez, former Director of Presidential Quality Management

My career began as a researcher for the department of the navy in San Diego, California and later in the office of the undersecretary of the navy in Washington. I was hired to lead the first Office for Presidential Quality Management at the White House Communications Agency. After a few years, I joined the White House Military Office (WHMO) where I serve as director of the customer support and organizational development directorate. In my role, I traveled with the president and supported many missions all over the world. I met Glenn on a presidential trip during the Clinton administration. He had worked in the transportation unit and eventually worked in my office in WHMO.

I had the honor of emceeing Glenn's retirement ceremony, which was an extraordinary event, filled with heartfelt testimonials by principals from the democratic and republican administrations. On that day, as we were heading out to the conference room, we were still receiving faxes and emails from cabinet members whose letters of congratulations we could not include in the ceremony given the high volume of commendations and high number of attendees. That is a testament to Glenn's capacity to interact with people at all levels and his natural gift to leave an indelible mark in their lives.

Glenn is incredibly loyal. He is someone you want to bring with you when the stakes are high. He's great at continually building his social network and establishing enduring relationships. He has instinctive political skills. He is direct, assertive and effective in his communications. He can tell you things in a very candid way without being disrespectful, but he never gives you room to misinterpret what he means. He uses plain text and always speaks truth to power. What he brings to an organization is his commitment to the mission. He puts the mission above himself and is the quintessential team player. He is also committed to advancing the organizational goals.

One thing I learned about Glenn was that you never knew where you would end up when he asked you about what you were doing on a particular weekend? I always responded "nothing" because I knew that his option was always better than any plans that I had. We attended concerts, fund raisers, and even spent casual time at President Clinton's house in Chappaqua, New York.

In my role as business school professor, executive coach and consultant, I deal with executives from corporations to government agencies. I'm exposed to all of it. Glenn's makeup is really unique. His wisdom and keen intuition transcends any degree. I'm proud of Glenn and I'm honored to have him as a friend.

Kay Torpey, former White House Stenographer

I'm originally from England and lived there on and off for fifteen years before coming to the states. My route to the White House was unexpected. At the time, my brother was a cameraman for CNN and had heard there was a job opening for a stenographer. He thought it would suit me perfectly. He called and asked if I was interested and of course, I was.

My employment at the White House was on a contractual basis for a court reporting company. I worked full-time as a stenographer for a couple of years, and then continued to fill in for a few years on a part-time basis when they needed extra help. It was an honor to work at the White House. Many people don't realize that the stenographers have been a part of the White House for a long time. All recent presidents have had them.

My role as a stenographer included recording and transcribing the press briefings and the pool reports. Glenn was already working on the press plane when I arrived. My first impression of Glenn was the same impression I hold of him today. He was kind, joyful, helpful, and always had a smile on his face. One of my fondest memories is of the "SEATO" game that we played on the press plane. We all wrote our seat numbers on a dollar bill, and put it into a pillowcase. I don't know who came up with the game, but we all enjoyed it. Glenn would get on the PA system and announce the winning numbers. I remember when Glenn was promoted to AFI. I was happy for Glenn but sad for us on the press plane because we wouldn't get to see him as much.

Glenn worked hard and in my mind, everyone appreciated him. He seemed to enjoy the trips and made the most of every moment. Even when we landed somewhere in the middle of the night and nearly everyone was asleep at the hotel, Glenn and his crew would be driving through the city in the middle of the night to deliver our equipment before the workday began. If we were in a foreign country, they would also watch for the local McDonalds!

Darryl Turner, Security Manager, White House Military Office
I was born in Roanoke, Virginia, and attended school there before going into the military. I worked as chief of staff in the Pentagon's security office. The point of contact and recruiter for the White House military Lt. Colonel Carmen Powell happened to work in my of-

fice. She mentioned one day that the White House was looking for an administrative person with security experience. She suggested I should apply for it. I did, and got the job. I was scared half to death and could not imagine what it would be like working at the White House. I had just returned from Germany, which I greatly enjoyed. I recalled that Germany was a very clean country, the way the United States was at one time.

I met Glenn in the White House military office. He was working in the transportation office at that time. My first impression of Glenn Powell was that he was domineering and overpowering but also a person who always gets the job done. While he wasn't necessarily the person at the center of attention, he always somehow got attention. Glenn is lots of things. He is strong willed, but he also always acts with integrity. He has great leadership skills, and is loyal to the very end.

As much as he loved his job, one of Glenn's greatest regrets is spending so much time away from his family, because deep down he is a family man, and loves his family more than anything. Glenn's guiding principle was to work hard and give every job his very best. One of the things that's most important to him is doing a good job as a father and husband. He works hard at that.

I recall our trip to Hope, Arkansas for the opening of the president's childhood home. Dr. Suarez, James Ross, Glenn and I were all riding in this vehicle on the way back from the opening. We went across a tollbooth and the clerk really had a bad attitude.

Glenn decided that she needed a new job. Dr. Suarez, who is a PhD and leadership development expert asked Glenn how he came to that conclusion. Glenn replied that he had an HSD (high school diploma), and his assessment was based on that experience!

I consider Glenn a brother. There is virtually nothing that Glenn could ask of me that I wouldn't try to do. He is the epitome of what a man should be.

Ken Wilson, former White House Employee, Military

I was born in San Francisco and I spent my childhood there and in Washington State. In 1982, the army assigned me to the White House to work as a chauffeur under the Reagan Administration. Eventually, I began working on AF1. Those were remarkable times, not without challenges. You encounter a multitude of personalities on AF1. Looking back, one of my funniest stories was about a severe dressing down that I received from a tiny 5'3" woman. One of my drivers had misplaced a box of chocolates that the woman had received as a gift. Another one of my drivers eventually found her box of chocolates under a spare tire. I had to personally take the box of chocolates to her and listen to her lecture me for I don't know how long.

I was Glenn's supervisor for three years, beginning in 1991. He was an excellent driver for the transportation department. A lot had changed in the city's layout from when I arrived in 1982 and when Glenn arrived in 1991. After the 1992 election, many of the older drivers retired, and there were a lot of changes.

Glenn was self-assured and talkative. He would walk into a room full of people and immediately become the center of attention. I didn't have a lot of contact with workers on the other shifts, so I called each individual in to meet them to discover if there was anything going on that I needed to know about. Right away, I got the impression that Glenn was head-and-shoulders above his colleagues. He was a great go -to person and organizer.

I was responsible for talking Glenn into taking the job traveling with the president aboard AF1. There were two men already traveling with the first family, but one of them injured his back. Glenn was hesitant to take the job. He loved working with his crew on the press plane and didn't want to transfer.

The Transportation Director Mr. Borden, was hesitant about Glenn taking on that level of responsibility and working directly with the president. I worked to convince him that Glenn was right for the job, while also trying to convince Glenn to take the job. Eventually, everybody got on board and Glenn went to work on AF1. When you work in close proximity to the president, you have to become a real company man. Glenn's wife, Ronda, had to take up a lot of slack at home because of Glenn's schedule. Over the years, Glenn had the burden of fitting his schedule around that of three presidents. Mr. Reagan and Mr. Bush stuck to their schedules. With Mr. Clinton, you had to be ready for swift schedule changes. Glenn had to be ready for last-minute calls that he was needed for flight to a foreign country. It was extremely unpredictable and the main reason I quit traveling.

Glenn was one of the ones I knew I could count on. I threw all kinds of assignments at him to test him. He passed every test with flying colors. Glenn never cut corners or straddled the rules. He was focused, above board, and could work unsupervised. He thinks outside of the box. Glenn could also find humor in almost anything no matter what was going on. Glenn was the only non-commissioned military personnel below the rank of sergeant major to receive a Legion of Merit award, which is the highest peacetime award you can receive. He was also the only White House military employee to receive a live video from the president and attendance by the first lady at his retirement.

Dr. Marshall Williams, former White House Employee

I was raised in Washington, D.C. I joined the military at the age of seventeen. I had the opportunity to go to college on a scholarship, but I had never known anyone who had done so successfully. I chose a military career, something I'd always wanted, and something I loved. One of the reasons is that I met my wife in the military. I retired in 2001 and had a couple of careers in corporate America, including my role as an executive director of Military Affairs for Home, Savings & Trust Mortgage.

I met Glenn Powell in the military in the INSCON in Fort Belvoir, Virginia. Given his welcoming spirit, I'm sure I just walked up and introduced myself. We became friends immediately. He would eventually become a colleague and a mentor.

To describe Glenn in one word, I will have to choose outstanding. It's rare to find someone who is all of these things – an outstanding soldier, businessman, family man, father, husband, and friend. Most people don't live up to all of them. You can trust Glenn with every secret this nation has, which is the reason so many people love him. They know how important it is to have people around you who are trustworthy… people with ethics. My only regret is that I don't have Glenn working with me now.

Of course we've all changed over the years, but Glenn's changes have come about after reaching an apex in his life – after traveling the world, seeing and experiencing things that others will never be able to see or experience, interacting with world leaders. I think Glenn now probably looks back and says, 'There should have been no way a kid from Toledo should have lived this life.'

One of my most memorable experiences with Glenn is when he went to bat for this young soldier in the White House who was experiencing some problems in her job. Glenn asked if I would talk with her because he simply believed in this individual. After talking to her, I also believed in this person's integrity, and wrote a favorable statement on her behalf. Two months later, she was vindicated, and this changed her life. The point is, this young woman confided in Glenn because no one else would give her the time of day. Glenn doesn't mind getting his hands dirty. This woman is now doing wonderful things in the congressional arena.

The attributes that made Glenn's life successful include the fact that he is a family man, which is hard when you've had the positions he's held. Also, there is his adaptability which helped him adjust to his surroundings so he could accomplish his success; his leadership skills, his integrity and overall kind spirit. All of these values have remained the staples of who Glenn Powell truly is.

Part Eleven

MEMORIES FROM MILITARY COLLEAGUES AND CHILDHOOD FRIENDS

Jiles Bayne, Close Friend, Fellow Soldier

I was born in Burlington, North Carolina, which is known for its cotton textile industry. I joined the military in 1977, and spent fifteen years with the army. I did a tour in Germany and was stationed in Fort Eustice in Virginia when I returned. The first time I met Glenn was when he got assigned to a unit I was already assigned to. We both became leader soldiers with part-time jobs as security officers.

I remember a time when we were stationed in Virginia and had a lieutenant there who was the executive officer of the unit. He was causing trouble for everyone. One day we had a meeting with the first sergeant, and Glenn stood up and told the first sergeant that this executive officer was causing problems. Then, he proceeded to tell the first sergeant that either he goes or we would go. Now, none of us knew Glenn was going to be so bold, but it worked. Most importantly, I don't think this guy was actually giving Glenn the same hard time he was giving everyone else, but Glenn saw us as a team and spoke out on behalf of the team.

I think both Glenn and I always wanted to be drill sergeants. We loved the idea of leading people and being in charge. When it didn't happen, Glenn came up with something called weekend training for new soldiers where he would educate them about being the best soldier they could be. Glenn figured out that the best way to discipline a soldier is take away their free time. It actually worked!

Glenn is awesome as a person and in how he balanced work and family. I got the opportunity to meet his mother once, and I saw where Glenn gets a lot of his love of family. Glenn is a great people person who is kind when he doesn't have to be.

Roberto Delgado, Career Soldier, Motor Vehicle Operator/Transportation Coordinator

I grew up in the South Bronx of New York City, and my family still lives there. I left home to enter the army in 1983. Glenn and I met in 1987 in Fort Eustis, Virginia. Glenn has always been serious about his work, and we always found a way to find humor in things.

I can tell you he was an excellent driver. We both drove early on in our army career. Glenn worked with a trucking company in Germany and drove a M915 tractor trailer company. Back then, our career field was known as a 64C (64 Charlie), which was a designated name for a motor vehicle operator. That later changed to the 88M (88 Mike). Glenn ended up being a driving instructor for a while.

Glenn has always been a loyal and trustworthy friend to me. We both told each other years ago that if we ever needed each other, no matter where we were, we'd be there for each other. Thank goodness, we've never had to act on that but he is a good friend. Everywhere I've been, we have kept in touch and been a support to each other.

When Glenn and I met we were both in trouble, though not in a bad way. It turned out that we both had orders to go to Germany, but we were both scheduled for a two-month basic non-commissioned officers course. Since they were offering the training in

Virginia, they didn't want to waste the money sending us over to Germany and back when we could do the training right there.

When Glenn and I showed up at 5:00 a.m. for the training, the sergeant major told us we were late and they weren't taking anymore soldiers. Of course, the fact was they were overbooked, but we had our paperwork so they had to take us. They assigned us to a janitor's closet. The room had been a bedroom before, but they had converted it to a janitor's closet. The sergeant major told us we had to fix that closet up and stay there through the training. Well, we ended up fixing it up and enjoying being there because they forgot to take the "janitors closet" sign off the door, and when they did the wake-up call every morning, they skipped us and so every morning we slept an hour later than everyone else. Unfortunately, when they found out they made us leave the barracks, because they decided to give our newly converted room to the new soldiers arriving for the next class. We stayed at our own homes and commuted in to the classes every morning.

Glenn and I ended up stationed in Manheim, Germany just a few weeks apart. Glenn got there before I did, and when I got there, he showed me around. We lived just a few miles away from each other. Glenn told me about a girl he had met and wanted to introduce her to me. That's how I met Ronda, we found out that our birthdays where on the same day. I liked her right away and we have been like brother and sister since then. Ronda is a great part of the team!

I was supposed to be assigned to the White House, but when Glenn and other friends told me how many hours were required and how I wouldn't have time for family, I turned it down. I think that was the only time I turned down an assignment and I did it for my family.

I attended Glenn's retirement ceremony in 2002, which was quite an event. Glenn has been a great friend and brother. It is said that when you PCS (permanent change of station) from a tour of duty knowing a good friend, that was a great tour. Well I'm here to tell you that I have had many great tours knowing my friend Glenn Powell for over twenty-nine years.

Danny Hudson, Military Colleague, Friend, Aspiring Music Producer and Songwriter

I was born in Newnan, Georgia, twenty-five miles south of Atlanta. I joined the military in 1979, after high school. I spent three years in Germany teaching computer programming and instruction. In 1988, I was stationed at Fort Belvoir in Virginia. That's where I met Glenn.

At first, Glenn and I had absolutely nothing in common. I was an athlete who played a lot of ball. I asked him three questions: Do you play ball? Do you party? Do you drink? He answered no to all of those. On top of that, I discovered that Glenn was a rules man. He didn't believe in bending or breaking the rules, while I was someone who was likely to live on the edge. None of us had any money when we were in the military, but Glenn and I had this ritual.

We would go to Church's Chicken every day and get a two-piece dinner, and on Fridays, we'd get chicken wings.

Glenn was definitely a momma's boy. I went to Toledo a couple times and met everyone. His family confirmed my suspicions. I also went to Cleveland and met Ronda's family. I can't put my finger on how, but Glenn and I became best friends. I ended up being his best man at his wedding. I had met Ronda when she was stationed in New Jersey. Glenn and I would drive up there to visit for the weekend. They would go out and I was the babysitter. One night, when they got back, I had fallen asleep while the baby was playing in the middle of the floor. That didn't go over too well.

As friends, Glenn and I were the odd couple. I was the administrative, communications man, while Glenn was the soldier. Whenever he needed to write an important letter, he would get me to write it. We used to laugh about how all that changed around when he went to the White House and started working for the president and riding on AF1. One of the things I'm proudest of was the time when the president flew into Dobbins Air Force Base and Glenn set up an AF1 tour for me.

Terry Pritchett, Childhood Friend

I have known Glenn for probably forty years. We grew up just five houses apart, but I didn't really meet him until we were in high school. When I was a junior and Glenn was a sophomore, we began to hang out together some and became friends.

Even as a young person, Glenn worked hard. He was the only one in our age group who had a real job. At the age of sixteen, he was a store manager and recommended his boss hire me. I got the job on Glenn's word. We worked at that store for almost three years. Seeing his work ethic completely changed the way I conducted myself. Glenn's family relationships helped shape the type of person he became. His mother was always his biggest supporter, always in his corner. Glenn showed her respect. Theirs was one of the few households where a teenage son wasn't giving his mother a bunch of problems.

Glenn did well for himself in the military. I remember living in California when my sister called and told me Glenn was on the news escorting President Clinton off AF1! I was floored that someone I knew was working that closely with the President, but I wasn't surprised at all that it was Glenn.

After traveling all over the world, Glenn is more worldly in that his conversation has broadened. He has great stories. It's interesting to see him so in touch with that bigger world. More so, it has always made me proud that he would come back home, humble as always, never forgetting his friends. I haven't shared this with Glenn, but I'm hoping to find a way to honor him, in the city of Toledo, and at the school he attended.

Part Twelve

CLINTON WHITE HOUSE PRESIDENTIAL APPOINTEES

Betty Currie, President Clinton's Personal Secretary

I grew up in the suburbs of Illinois, though my roots are in Mississippi. I have had a long and wonderful career in public service, beginning with my work at the Department of the Navy, and other agencies, including the Peace Corps where I worked for the Peace Corps director and for the Africa Region. My work with Peace Corps afforded me several trips to Africa. When my first marriage ended in divorce, my daughter and I remained in Washington. After retiring for the first time, I continued to work part-time in various capacities. When President Clinton began his campaign in 1992, I volunteered to work and even moved to Little Rock where I became Warren Christopher's secretary. In 1993, I was asked by President Clinton to serve as his personal secretary. I was one of the first people there and saw many of the new appointees come through that door. My husband Robert and I are now enjoying our retired status – my second retirement. I volunteer when I find a cause I can't say no to.

I met Glenn on AF1, and my first thought was... impressive. Over the years, we became both friends and colleagues. He is dependable, outgoing, and a non-gossiper! On one of our foreign trips on AF1, I wanted to go downstairs to get something from my bag. Glenn said I couldn't go, but that he would go for me. He said he was doing it that one and final time, and I couldn't tell anyone! The two attributes that best define Glenn Powell are honesty and generosity. He was always, always willing to help.

Michael Duga, former Clinton White House Staff

I'm from Florida, and was just twenty years old when I went to work for President Clinton' and Mrs. Clinton in 1996. I think I was one of the youngest staffers on his team. One of the people I worked closely with during the Clinton years was Kirk Hanlin, White House Trip Director. We continued to work together after the Clinton years, including our work on the confirmation of then Senator Chuck Hagel, who became secretary of defense. I later learned that Kirk was second only to the president and Bruce Lindsey in the number of times he rode on AF1 between 1993 and 2001.

After my stint with the Clinton Administration, I served as chief of staff to a U.S. senator. That was during the same time that Glenn was working for Senator Clinton. I later served as policy advisor to the Department of Defense under President Obama. Amazingly, Glenn and my paths have crossed many, many times; but we still haven't met in person. Glenn was known by just about everyone as one of the gems within the White House. When he fell ill, there was an outpouring of caring from people all over. Someone sent out this mass email around the world about Glenn's serious illness. Kirk sent me a note saying, "Do whatever you can."

Thanks to that network of caring, Glenn ended up in the VIP area of the Soldiers Field Hospital, which is the area for presidents of the United States. We all pushed for that because it was Glenn and he was worth the effort.

For whatever reason, we were able to have a medical staffer in Glenn's room. I don't remember much of that day. It was very long and very cold out. I remember inquiring about Walter Reed's transportation process between Glenn's room and the site where his surgery would take place. Kirk Hanlin texted me in the seventeenth hour of that day and asked if we needed to talk. We didn't. He was getting my updates in real time to pass along and I was doing the same to Doug Band.

I knew that Glenn had traveled all over the world hundreds of hours with President Clinton, and they considered him part of the family. I was the one who kept a tight rope on everything that was going on and letting the president know regularly how he was. Someone like Glenn Powell, you just want to move heaven and earth to make things work.

Kris Engskov, Personal Aide to President Clinton

Glenn and I first met in the White House travel office in 1994. He was one of the first people I met when I started. I was responsible for all the press bags. Glenn and I worked together hand and hand for two years. He was a real team player. He was very welcoming, and spent a lot of time telling me what had worked for him and what had not worked. In other words, he gave great instructions on how to navigate.

We sat on many, many airplanes together. He kept it very real, and he did not get caught up in non-sense. The president liked him a lot, and accepted him as part of the family, and Glenn knew how to fit into the family.

I recall once when we were in Moscow, we got up at 1:00 a.m. and loaded up an old Russian truck in the dead of morning to get the bags loaded on the plane. When we finally got to the tarmac, we found out that that the plane was locked up. Glenn asked for a screwdriver. He unlatched the bottom of the press charter plane, and we climbed up the ladder to first class. That was Glenn Powell. He was a can-do guy and strategic thinker. He would get the job done.

Sharon Farmer, former Director, Office of White House Photography

I met Glenn when I came to the White House and he was the driver for the staff support van. Usually that van included the military aide, the medical staff, and me. Glenn was like a mother hen when he worked. You could tell that he studied people, situations, and possible outcomes. He did his homework, and kept a "can do" attitude. He was the complete package. Anyone can run a crew. Glenn led a team. His team refused to be anything but top notch. He never lost travelers' luggage, and he was smart enough to work around personalities. Glenn was also funny back then. He could find humor in the most mundane thing.

I will remember this one incident until the day I die. There was this high-level staff member who was in the support van with us while we were traveling in upstate New York, who spoke disparagingly of women, calling them the "B" word. Besides me, there were other women in the van. Glenn politely asked him if he had a mother or a sister. That told me something about Glenn. He is professional to the bone, but he also has personal values that he lives by. The planet could use more men like Glenn. It would be a better world. He's a friend you keep for life.

Kirk Hanlin, former Special Assistant to the President and Trip Director

I guess you could call me a serial political operative. I've worked in more political campaigns than I'd like to admit, beginning with Walter Mondale and ending with Obama. When I heard in 1991 that Bill Clinton was running for president, I decided he could win, and called Mark Gearan who I knew was working on pulling a political team together. He arranged for me to meet Governor Clinton. One of the things that was important to me was to hear him speak. I did, and he was fabulous. I went on the road the next day coordinating rallies, town hall meetings, bus trips, even the Arsenio Hall show. I didn't have a day off until after the 1992 convention where I was his lead advance. I then worked straight through Election Day where again I was his lead. For the transition and first four years of his administration, I was lead advance on both domestic and international trips. I was lead advance for election night in the 1996 campaign, and not long after that I was chosen by President Clinton to be his trip director. I was in that job for the final four years of his administration.

I met Glenn after I became trip director. We traveled on over one thousand flights on AF1 together. I remember talking to White House aides Andrew Friendly and Kelly Craighead to get a rundown on everyone I'd need to work with in my new job. They both said the same things about Glenn: He's a super nice guy; he'll make your job easier; he is a consummate professional; he's a quick study; he's always in a good mood. Everything they told me turned out to be true and more.

Most people don't even think about the responsibility of keeping luggage in place and delivered at the end of a trip, and that's because Glenn and his team were so good at what they did, you didn't have to give it a second thought. Travelers on AF1 would simply leave their bag in a room at the White House and it would magically appear in their hotel room anywhere in the world. Glenn made sure the president's staff could focus on their jobs and not spend one second worrying about luggage. Everyone knew Glenn would take care of them.

I recall the first time we saw the movie, *Air Force One*, we were in Los Angeles. The studio was just releasing the film to theatres and gave us a VHS copy to watch. The president said to show it in the conference room and invite the staff and key crew to watch. In the movie itself, there are scenes when everyone is held hostage in the AF1 conference room, which made watching the movie from that room surreal. First Dana Petard the president's military aide made a comment about something in the movie regarding the fictional military aide. Then, when it gets to the part where Harrison Ford goes down to the luggage "berth" to look for a satellite cell phone, Glenn piped up and said, "Oh, no...my luggage is never all piled up like that!" We all laughed including the president because we knew Glenn was right.

There were a few times when I asked Glenn about certain people's bags. Not only could he tell you from memory how many pieces there were, he could describe each bag in detail. If a passenger needed something from their luggage, Glenn could go directly to the bag in flight without a second thought. Oftentimes we would time our flights so that we'd arrive early in the morning so that the president and staff could have a full day's work on arrival. We would usually be dressed somewhat casually with blue jeans and t-shirts for the red eye flight. When you went on board, Glenn would ask what luggage you needed for the morning. He would literally make sure we had the luggage with the appropriate clothing sitting next to us when we woke up to prepare for the next morning.

Glenn was always a professional in his job. Not just ensuring everyone received their baggage but when we traveled, keeping us straight on what and how much we could and could not bring back on the plane. Something most people might not know is that President Clinton was the most traveled President in United States history. Glenn Powell was on almost every single one of those record setting trips.

What Glenn brought to the table for the president, the White House, and what he would bring to any organization is the intellectual capacity to organize things in his mind that you wouldn't think of yourself. He supports others so that they are in a better position to perform.

Ben Johnson, Assistant to the President, Director, One America Initiative

"I was born in Arkansas, but grew up in Fort Bend, Indiana. I went to the military shortly after high school and later moved to Washington, D.C. in the seventies.

I worked for D. C. Mayor Marion Barry and then for the City of D.C. My wife, Jackie, just recently retired from the U.S. Department of Labor. Like so many other people, once we came to Washington, we couldn't imagine living anywhere else.

I joined the Clinton Administration in 1993. My first job was with the Office of Public Liaison, headed by Alexis Herman. When she left to take over as Secretary of Labor, I was promoted to assistant to the president, and director of the Office of One America, the president's race initiative. I held that job through the remainder of his Administration.

The first time I met Glenn was during my first flight on AF1. There were a number of us traveling with the president to Memphis, Tennessee including Ernie Green, Lottie Shackelford, Alexis Herman, Carol Willis and me. That was September 1993, when the president gave that most memorable speech to the COGIC (Church of God in Christ) Convocation. What I remember about Glenn being on that trip was that he had an answer for everything we asked him. We hadn't flown before and simply didn't know the protocol for flying with the president. Glenn explained everything to us, including the difference between the secure and non-secure telephones which were available to staff and traveling guests of the president. He noted that one phone was brown and the other phone was red. It was eye opening for me to have this young black guy educating us about something so important to the presidency.

It seemed like I'd known Glenn forever when I met him. He knew exactly what to do to make you feel at ease, as if you were the most important person in the world at that moment. What a guy! He was so good at what he did, and he always did it with a smile. I recall during one of the president's trips to Africa that we were in Nigeria at a state dinner. While there, President Mandela called President Clinton from Tanzania to tell him he believed he had a peace agreement between the warring factions of Congo. We quickly changed our travel plans and flew to Tanzania. I remember that Glenn is the person who made that quick transition work for everyone. He treated everyone with so much respect, and at the same time, we were secure that everything that needed to be taken care of was being taken care of.

A not-so pleasant memory of traveling on AF1 is losing my White House pass. When I reported it to the security office, I was not only asked to write a lengthy report but I was also made to feel as if I had been negligent. I was pretty angry. When I called back to the office, I learned that they'd found my pass. It had somehow gotten stuck between the seats. When I mentioned this to Glenn, he explained that it was no big deal, and that this was a frequent occurrence. From that moment on, I had a great deal of respect for Glenn. No matter what kind of roadblocks were put in his way, he found a way around them.

His honesty and kindness is an attribute that is almost natural. One of the kindest people I've met. More than anything, I have a great deal of respect for Glenn Powell, and had a close bond with him both because of his role at the White House but also because of our military careers. We try to stay in touch. Glenn is the world's best at checking in to make sure things are good.

Michele Kreiss, former Clinton White House Advance Team Leader

My home is Maryland, and I've always had my finger in politics, but never to the extent that I did with the Clinton campaign. I got my feet wet in campaign advance work when Jerry Brown ran his first presidential race, and I did his advance in Maryland. It was fun. Around 1993, when my youngest son moved back to Washington to work with my family's printing company, I saw it as a time to do what I wanted to do. What was exciting about this campaign was that Bill and Hillary were my peers and stood for the very things I'd always believed in. I started volunteering whenever I could.

It was Isabel Tapia Wilson who worked at the White House Office of Scheduling and Advance who said the campaign really needed more mature workers on the road. I thought I might be too old. She wasn't hearing that, and sent me to Janesville, Wisconsin to do advance. So far, I've kept my promise to my family to not go back on the road again. Not sure I could do nineteen hours with cold pizza and the endless stress of political advance work.

Most of my interaction with Glenn during the Clinton years was during the international trips. I did a lot of overnights and I can tell you that Glenn Powell does not sleep. There are people we work with who you simply have to say 'here's what I need done,' and they take it from there. Glenn was one of the ones. His military background has helped instruct the way he handles complicated situations. No doubt he faced frustrating situations, but I never saw him lose it.

After eight years doing advance in the Clinton Administration, my body paid me back. I had a silent heart attack. Shortly after that, I accepted an assignment in Nova Scotia as an independent contractor with former White House colleague Debi Schiff's events company. It was my first flight away from home after learning about my silent heart attack. I didn't know until I got there that Glenn was working with her too. When I saw Glenn I burst into tears. I felt safe. He was my buddy in a foxhole.

When we learned that Glenn was in the hospital, over at Walter Reed, we immediately got on the Internet and let all of his White House friends know that he was going through this horrible health scare. It was amazing the people who reached out and made things happen. Glenn had no idea he was being placed in the same area of the hospital that presidents are placed. We let President Clinton know as well because we knew he would want to reach out to Ronda and the family. To let you know how important Glenn is to us, there was a military person posted outside Glenn's hospital room who we told without hesitation that Glenn needed to be treated special.

Glenn, today, is a more mellow version of the Glenn who worked in the White House environment, simply because he's not jumping into airplanes. Like all of us, the stress he had to handle was much more than we really realized. Ronda came up to Halifax to work with us, and it was so heartwarming to see them together. They are such a loving couple. They are an awesome couple and family.

Mark Lindsey, Assistant to the President, Director of Operations

I was born in Cleveland, and I came to the White House to take over the Office of White House Operations during President Clinton's second term. I had worked as counsel to Congressman Louise Stokes (D-OH) for a number of years, and I was one of the few people who had no history with the Clintons but knew a number of people who did. I think they reached out to me solely based on my past work experience.

I met Glenn through Colonel Jake Simmons, whose office reported to me. Unlike Colonel Simmons and Glenn, I do not have a military background. I had actually heard about Glenn before I became an assistant to the president. Glenn had an amazing reputation. Colonel Simmons had nothing but positive things to say about him, so I guess I already had high expectations of Glenn. Everything people said about him turned out to be true.

Glenn is a professional, and although some of that can be attributed to his military training, much of it is just who Glenn is. Glenn is even professional in the way that he tells you that you did something stupid. Everyone took things better when they came from Glenn, which was essential in his role because he dealt with people from all backgrounds and levels. Glenn is a great leader who transcended any labels regarding his areas of proficiency. He brought personal qualities to work, and I'm certain he took the skills he used at work to his home.

Lt. Colonel Alphonso Maldon, retired Colonel and former Director, White House Military Office

I was born in Florida, and my father was in the military, so I guess I followed in his footsteps when I decided to join the military and make it my life career. My last duty assignment before retiring was on Capitol Hill working on legislative military affairs.

We selected Glenn to join the White House Transportation Agency, which reported to me. Glenn brought the kind of leadership, results-oriented work ethics that an employer always looks for in staff. Besides that, people liked him a lot. He started out in transportation and did logistics.

Glenn was like our officer-in-charge, one of those people who was the go-to guy. I would always say to Leroy Borden, head of the transportation agency, 'we wanted Glenn on this trip, on AF1.' I asked Glenn to do it, and I didn't have to worry about it. I had great respect for Glenn; his work ethics, his dependability and his attitude to do whatever it took to get the job done. I've had the opportunity to lead and manage many people over my forty-five-year work career. Glenn is at the top of that list. If I've got a tough job I'd like Glenn at the helm. I'd go so far as to say that

Glenn was the glue that held the CARPET family together during our time there, but also after we left. He made sure we found a way to give back to families and children, then later made sure we all came together after we retired from our roles at the White House.

I remember our Africa trip in 1997. Glenn and I would have our logistics meetings late at night, before and during a foreign trip. We'd go over everything to the last detail. One standard rule was that everyone traveling with the president had to leave their luggage outside their doors before midnight, and they would have to be on the bus at a certain time on the morning of departure.

In this one instance, a congresswoman's luggage was unaccounted for, so I asked Glenn to get the key, go into the room and retrieve the luggage. It turned out that the luggage was there, but so was she. She gave Glenn a hard time for entering her room. Glenn remained calm and collected in spite of that. He has this attitude of wanting to please everyone. He never lost his calm. He was always concerned about the bigger picture being that his actions and reactions reflected on the president. Of course, he could have said that I sent him to the room, but he didn't. He took responsibility for making the judgment call.

The attributes I believe have benefitted Glenn the most throughout his life and his career are his humility and his honesty. I never got the idea that he was dishonest. Mistakes were made, but he never tried to hide them. Those are the values you grow up with that become part of your DNA.

Thurgood Marshall, former White House Director, Cabinet Affairs

I grew up in New York City and Washington, D.C., went to law school at the University of Virginia. I began my legal career clerking for a federal judge and then worked in a D.C. law firm, and eventually worked for then-Senator Al Gore. I worked on the Clinton Presidential Campaign and came to the White House to work in Vice President Gore's legislative affairs office. I'd known the vice president over the years and had great respect for him and his father, the late Senator Gore. During President Clinton's second term, I was named cabinet secretary and directed the White House Office of Cabinet Affairs, replacing Kitty Higgins.

I actually met Glenn early on during my time at the White House. Our very first meeting was actually standing under a wing of AF1 on a tarmac. Someone from his fan club introduced me to him. It was obvious that everyone thought very highly of him, but I didn't really get to know him well until I began traveling with the President. After Glenn and I traveled on a few trips together, I found out that what the fan club was trying to tell me about Glenn was true. He is a pretty special guy. It turned out that I traveled a lot, both domestic and international. My role as cabinet affairs director required me to be around to brief the President, be a go-between, and serve as a resource when the president traveled. Glenn and I became good friends during that time.

Glenn is a centered, dedicated, consummate professional, always delivering at least one hundred twenty percent. He never missed a step. I found it truly amazing. I traveled many places with Glenn, but I could never tell whether he was under stress. He was always so unflappable. I never once saw him give off any negativity. I marveled that Glenn was able to travel nonstop and look as good as he did. I tried to get my sons to see the value of that...if they could try to master that steadiness, take it to that next level, and perform.

To top it off, Glenn did everything he did without a cheat sheet. He was a fast learner. He represented all the good things we wish for in uniformed staff. The "Glenns" of the world don't receive the credit they deserve most of the time because they make their work look effortless. Somewhere, though, he invariably found the right switches...whether he had to work to find them, or whether he simply enhanced them.

Mack Mclarty, Chief of Staff to President Clinton, Ambassador to the Americas

I first met Glenn on an AF1 assignment. He took over the job from Sergeant Bob Lehman. I was immediately drawn to his warm and friendly yet still proper military demeanor. I instantly knew that he was a person that you could count on, and he would do his job in a way that made it easy for you to like and trust him.

Every AF1 trip I took with the president, I would see Glenn during that trip. You'd get off the plane and Glenn would make things easier for you wherever you landed. Glenn has a natural and proven ability to make any endeavor or business better than what they are. He is loyal, takes pride in what he does, and is good-hearted. Glenn is a contributor and doer with high energy, and he knows how to channel that energy in whatever he does. If he's interested, he's thought about it completely through before taking action. I think it is interesting that Glenn served under both Bushes, as well as President Clinton.

Minyon Moore, former White House Assistant to the President, and Director of the Political Office
I grew up in Chicago, Illinois and worked for a number of years in local politics there. I worked directly with another great politician and civil rights leader, Jesse Jackson, before and after his presidential bid in 1988.

I came to the Clinton Administration in 1997 to head up the White House Political Office after Craig Smith, a longtime Clinton aide and friend, left for the private sector. I was one of the now-famous and historical African American assistant to President Clinton (historical because it was the first time a president had more than one African America assistant to the president – the top positions in the White House.) It was such an honor for me to work for President Clinton, but also an honor to serve the American people during that important time in history.

I think I met Glenn on AF1 during one of President Clinton's many trips around the country. What I remember best about first meeting him is his infectious smile. I noted very early that Glenn was unique: He treated us like his family, but didn't let "family," interfere with the job he had to do.

There are two things I expressly remember as I would observe Glenn on AF1: He never met a stranger. It didn't matter what level you happen to be, he made it his business to welcome you into the family. The other thing was he always treated everyone with dignity and respect. He interacted with more dignitaries than most people did, but he treated everyone the same. Part of that was his own sense of self. He exuded self-confidence. You knew he knew what he was doing. The other thing, I'm sure, was his spiritual grounding that teaches us, "Do unto others as you would have them do unto you."

The reason I really wanted to be included in this part of Glenn's book, is this: If I don't say anything else about this guy, I want to say, 'Thank you for being such a great public servant.' I know we were not the easiest people to deal with, but we just could not *not* be nice to Glenn. I'm just so grateful he was part of my life. That's why I wanted to do this. When he was sick, that sense that we might lose him had me a nervous wreck. I am forever grateful to Glenn Powell.

Helen Robinson, former Special Assistant for Personal Correspondence and Oval Office Operations

I grew up in Cotton Plant, Arkansas, but moved to California after school and became a military spouse. We traveled around the country and overseas during my husband's military career. We got orders for Jacksonville Air Force Base in Jacksonville, Arkansas. This move brought me back home after being away for eighteen years. It was a blessing in many ways, giving me the opportunity to reconnect with my family and to begin working for Governor Clinton. I worked for the Governor for several years before he ran for president. Around that time, we got orders to transfer to Pope Air Force Base in Fayetteville, North Carolina.

Shortly after Clinton became president, I received a call from a former work colleague, Nancy Hernreich, who offered me a position at the White House. I had worked with Nancy in Governor Clinton's office. I was hired as the special assistant for Personal Correspondence and Oval Operations.

My first day at the White House was the day that President Clinton and First Lady Hillary Clinton attended Jackie Kennedy's funeral. I was very excited to be there and to this day, I can remember everything that took place, including the dress I was wearing. I was held up in the security check point which meant that someone had to come over and escort me to the West Wing. Kelly Crawford from Oval Office Operations finally made it to my rescue. I reconnected with President Clinton, Nancy and other White House staffers and I met Betty Currie, President Clinton's personal secretary who was very nice and showed me the workings of the Oval Office. To this day Betty and I are still friends. Nancy Hernreich was my immediate supervisor. I also worked with Carolyn Huber, special assistant to President Clinton and the first family. We both know friends and family of the Clinton family. Carolyn worked with Mrs. Clinton at the Rose Law Firm. Carolyn introduced me to Glenn Powell.

One of Carolyn's roles was meeting and greeting President and Mrs. Clinton's personal guests, and escorting them to the residence. She had worked for a number of years with Mrs. Clinton in the Rose Law Firm. Glenn had come over to the White House from the department of the army, and one of his roles was to assist the first family with taking care of guests to the residency. After that meeting, I'd see Glenn quite regularly in the residence, or sometimes over in the West Wing. He was always pleasant. In time, he introduced me and the other Oval Office staff to his wife—who worked for the White House Military Office—and his two sons. They were an extremely attractive and pleasant family. After we left the Clinton Administration, we continued to keep in close contact.

After we both left the White House, I remember Glenn calling and checking in on me. He wouldn't want anything except to know that I was okay. We'd catch up on everyone, but it was always a good feeling to know that someone remembered you, and cared about how you were doing. Glenn is a trustworthy, hardworking man, and appreciative of the small things. He worked hard, but he had time to laugh too. Glenn also has a sense of fairness about him. I think that came from life experiences and to some extent the military.

Ron Saleh, former White House Staff

I became acquainted with the Clintons during the 1993 Inauguration. I was a volunteer who helped orchestrate that huge event. Later, I worked at the White House for a couple of different people in the East Wing. Actually, Mrs. Rodham (Mrs. Clinton's mother) recommended me to work on the inauguration, and afterwards I worked with Marsha Scott who worked in White House Presidential Personnel, then for one of Mrs. Clinton's aides, Carolyn Huber.

I met Glenn when he was working in CARPET. I needed to purchase audiovisual equipment for the office, so I ordered a car, and Glenn happened to be the driver. After that, anytime I needed a car, I'd ask for Glenn. He really helped me out. He knew a lot about audiovisual equipment. He was extremely helpful, always.

After the Clinton years, Glenn and his wife, Ronda worked with Debi Schiff, and I contracted with her to do a big project for the Canadian Minister of Defense, and that was how we reconnected. Glenn is a great manager, straightforward. Besides being a great manager, he is not afraid of hard work. If I had to choose one word to describe Glenn, it would be loyal. Glenn is a "whatever-it-takes" kind of guy. Having people like Glenn to work with is what made the Clinton Presidency a success.

Debra Schiff, former White House Receptionist, Oval Office Operations, The White House and Assistant Chief of Protocol, U.S. Department of State

I was born in California, but raised in Texas. I began working for the Clinton campaign in 1992 out of Dallas, Texas. I oversaw and managed the candidate's inflight services for the campaign charter plane from March through November 1992. I joined the White House on January 20, 1993, and was a member of the president's personal staff in the West Wing. I also traveled with the President and the White House Press Corps from 1993 to 1995.

Glenn was one of the first people I met when I started traveling with the president and press corps. Glenn would take care of everyone. It was always comforting just knowing there was someone like Glenn looking out for you. He would reassure me and many others that everything would be all right during sometimes very stressful trips. From the moment I met Glenn, we bonded and became friends forever. If Glenn liked you, he liked you one hundred percent, unconditionally. He was not only a good friend to me but to my husband, Jimmy, too.

After the Clinton Administration, Glenn has worked for me as a contractor. Glenn is caring, honest, and respectful. My team and clients have great respect for Glenn and they have come to love him as well!

From 1993 until we departed in 2001, Glenn and former director of the White House Military Office, John Gaughan, recruited White House staff to participate in the CARPET holiday party. My claim to fame was serving as the Christmas Elf, and giving out gifts to the staff and their family. The AF1 flight attendants were also recruited as Santa's helpers. Glenn is the only person I can think of who could have secured us to do that each and every year.

Something you knew about Glenn without him ever having to say, it was that he genuinely respected the office of the presidency. Glenn took his roles in serving the president seriously. He took it all very seriously. He respected everyone around him whether they were sweeping the floor or sitting at a desk making global decisions. I am honored to know Glenn Powell and his family!

Michael Teague, former Director of the White House Press Pool and Trip Coordinator for the White House Travel Office

I'm Arkansan, born and bred and got my first taste of politics when my dad ran for state senate when I was five or six years old. He was serving in the Arkansas state senate when he passed away and Governor Bill Clinton sat with our family on the front row at his funeral. So, when I had a chance to volunteer for the Clinton Campaign for President I jumped on it. I was still in college at the time. My first trip with the president was to Nashua, New Hampshire. Glenn was one of the main people I dealt with. There was also Rudy Cunningham and O'Neal Houck. I'd say ninety percent of the trips I took, these guys were with me. On domestic trips, there might be only two, but on international trips, there were usually four or five because of the size of the traveling press corps.

Kris Engskov started out as our travel office contact, and I remember one trip the president made to New Hampshire, Kris asked if I would do travel office advance for the traveling press and man the filing center. He told me that these guys called CARPET would be there to assist me. I didn't know what any of that meant and definitely didn't realize this was long-term. Soon after, Kris moved on to become director of the White House press pool, which opened a spot at the travel office for me. None of us could have done our job without the CARPET guys. At that time, Glenn was part of the CARPET crew.

Most of the time the White House press officers were in their own world focused on their jobs. However, once we got to where we were going there was not a single time that McCurry, Lockhart, Terranzo, Payne, Glynn and all the press office staff didn't each stop to personally thank Glenn and the CARPET crew for the work they did. They were phenomenal and made our jobs so much easier. I mean, if things went missing or something didn't get loaded, that was all their responsibility. I remember once we were in Russia and one of the major network correspondent's bags didn't get loaded onto the bus. We went all the way back to the airport, forty miles, then one of the CARPET guys found the bag in the bottom of the airplane. It had been there all along. No matter the circumstances we were representing the White House and the president so we kept a smile on our faces no matter what problem might pop up. We were dealing with the press. The CARPET guys were well aware of this too, and they were professional in every way.

There were some fun times too, especially getting to visit some of the foreign countries. When we'd go out to dinner, I would hang out with Glenn and his crew a lot of times. We'd have a few beers, de-stress. We'd talk about some of the more difficult situations we had to deal with. It took some finagling sometime to remain respectful and professional, but Glenn could do it better than anyone. I really respected him for that, because there were times when people would ask him to do something when they really shouldn't, but he would always know how to handle it.

While I think some of the CARPET staff that had been around a while and were just excited to be part of the White House crew, you could tell Glenn was destined for something more. He seemed to be the inspirational leader. Glenn was the personality, the ambassador.

I wasn't surprised when Glenn ended up being promoted to AF1 logistics. He was definitely AF1 material. It turned out we overlapped quite a bit then when Kris became the president's personal aide and I became the director of the pool.

On international trips, everyone knew how long they'd be flying so you'd try to grab sleep however and whenever you could get it because you knew when you landed, there would be no downtime for the rest of the day. For the longest time, I tried to figure out why it was that when everyone else was arriving to our destination, groggy-eyed, and exhausted from terrible sleep, Glenn shows up bright eyed and bushy-tailed, as refreshed as if he'd slept eight comfortable hours in a king sized bed. While everyone else was fighting to get in that tiny bathroom on AF1, Glenn was already washed up and dressed. What I found out over time was that once we took off from Andrews AFB in D.C., Glenn made himself a bed down in the "bowels of the plane" where the bags were. Few people even knew how to get down there, which is why it was the perfect sleeping area. Where staff comes out the backdoor of the plane...if you go in the opposite direction, there is a massive area where bags, a refrigerator, WHCA equipment, and all kinds of secret service paraphernalia was…and Glenn's bedroom!

One of my priorities was to ensure the press ate well. As long as I was in that role at the travel office, the press received plenty of good food during their trips. I finally convinced Sue Hazard, who was the director of the Travel Office and responsible for press travel that the food was a huge perk that would pay dividends. Previous administrations had treated the press like kings and queens, and it seemed to enhance the relationship with the White House. Sue finally agreed, and we slowly rebuilt that relationship. Glenn and his crew played a huge role in doing that, too.

Part Thirteen

POWELL FAMILY MEMBERS

Gloria Banks, Mother-in-Law

I grew up in Phoenix, Arizona, which is where Ronda was born. In Phoenix, we weren't exposed to the racial problems most of the country was experiencing because the majority of our population was Mexican and Indian. Ronda and I moved to Cleveland, Ohio in 1968 with my second husband, Larry. Our son Marcus was born in September 1969. My family was now complete. I still missed the Mexican food in Phoenix, but I learned to cook it myself. I retired from a hotel where I worked for over thirty years as a housekeeper. Since retirement, I have more time to bowl, dance, and skate. I'm also enjoying more time being a grandmother to Darius and Warren, and I think I'm a good grandmother. When Warren was born, I hadn't held a baby in a long time. I picked him up but soon handed him right back to Ronda because he was so tiny. I love it when my grandchildren come to visit Cleveland.

As a child, Ronda was serious about school from the time she was in elementary. All of her life, she was like my right hand. After I got used to her being gone to the military, my son, Marcus, joined the military.

I can honestly say that I liked Glenn from the first time I met him, and that is saying a lot because my daughter Ronda means the world to me. My intuition was right about Glenn. He's been a good husband and father. Glenn has been a good son-in-law too. I enjoy visiting Glenn and Ronda. He is a wonderful tour guide. We spend a lot of time touring Washington, D.C. when I visit and eating in nice restaurants. I believe that if anything should ever happen to my ex-husband and me, Glenn would step in and help pick up the pieces. I wouldn't trade him for the world.

Glenn is dedicated to his family and to his work. One of my best memories of Glenn was when we were at President Clinton's last Christmas party. Before the event, Glenn called and asked for my social security number. A newcomer on my job overheard my end of the conversation with Glenn. When she realized why I was providing the information, she shouted, "Oh, that's my man!" The next time that I went to work, I showed them my photos from the Christmas party. I was grinning from ear to ear. I was so proud of my son-in-law.

Larry Banks, Father-in-Law

I was born in Georgia but I have lived in Cleveland, Ohio since I was two years old. For over thirty years now, I have lived in the south suburbs of Cleveland, Euclid Heights. I am happily married and recently retired from my job as an environmentalist for the state of Cleveland.

Glenn married my daughter, Ronda, who is a one-of-a-kind young woman. Growing up, Ronda was an excellent student and never gave her mother and me any trouble. I do recall her always wanting to look three or four years older than whatever her age was. After high school, we had a conversation about college. She wanted to explore other options and decided to try the military.

The first time Ronda introduced Glenn to me, I thought he was an extraordinary young man, and I was especially impressed with his military background, as I had served in the Air Force. My first station was Luke Air Force Base, in Glendale, Arizona. I spent five years outside Paris and one year in Germany. I loved every minute of it, but left the military in 1967 because if you're away for seven years you have to renew your citizenship.

Both Ronda and Glenn went to the military because they believe in structure. She and Glenn are a lot alike. They both love their families and believe in doing well by others while never asking for anything in return. I couldn't have asked for a better man to entrust my daughter to. I know that when I leave this earth, she and the boys will be well taken care of by Glenn.

Eileen Belcher, Sister

I really enjoyed growing up in Toledo. As a child, there were lots of things to do. I remember we went to concerts and traveled to Michigan to shop. Later on, the city changed and jobs left. I didn't realize that until I moved away. All the factories and the local restaurants just disappeared. During the years that Glenn and I grew up, our parents were able to work and make a good living. There were lots of jobs in the factories, and other service jobs. When factories started sending jobs to other countries that hurt our city and our state.

Glenn was a mama's boy and could get away with all kinds of things that the rest of us couldn't. Even as a child he was always busy being his own person. When Glenn decided he was going to the army, he said he wasn't interested in going to college to get a career. The military would be his career. We had other family members in the military at the time. One thing we felt good about was that the military kept Glenn on the straight and narrow. Some of the young people in our hometown got mixed up in all kinds of things. I remember the Black Panthers headquarters were not far from where we lived, and they would pass out flyers. We didn't think much about it.

Our community had everything we needed. There was a movie theatre, grocery stores, churches, and Rudy's Hot Dog shop, which Glenn loved. My mother became the first black manager at Kroger. My sister and I also ended up working at Kroger. I only worked there for a short time, but she became a manager. My mother met many people in her line of work and forged friendship with folks of different ethnicities.

My first experience with prejudice was when I got a job at Elder Beerman, an Ohio-based department store that was part of Macy's. I worked there for fifteen years, including several years as manager. I was overworked and finally found another job that offered a better salary. The manager at a local finance company, Beneficial, offered me a job. I took it without knowing how many hats I'd be wearing. When I complained to my mother, she took me by the hand and told me 'if anyone here can do this job, you can do it, and better.' She said that even if I had to read the manager's directions twice or three times, I had to do that. Then, if I still didn't understand, I should go and ask the manager to explain it. She never took "no," or "I can't," for an answer.

Margaret Powell worked forty-three years for Kroger and received all kinds of awards. She made a difference there including making it possible for other blacks and other women to become managers. Most importantly, she made her children believe we could do anything whether we actually could or not. She was a very strong woman who taught me some important life lessons. She was a problem solver who did everything fairly. The store she managed was in the black community in the inner city of Toledo. She earned a lot of respect during her years with Kroger. Glenn is a lot like my mother in that any job he goes into he brings that happiness and positive attitude along with him. He makes his coworkers happy to come to work. He will do an outstanding job no matter what the job.

I also remember that we had this big burger grill. My brother and I would have to go downstairs and get hot dogs from the refrigerator and come back up and cook them on the grill. Glenn was so clumsy, though, he would fall down the stairs every time. We children would sing along with records, make up dance steps and sing to my mother just like they did on the Cosby Show. She would love that. We all loved our trips into Michigan where we would stop at White Castles to eat.

I moved to Jacksonville, Florida in 2004, following my sister. Our old community, Dorr Street, recently had a reunion. Plenty of people came. It was a mixed group. My mother turned eighty-years-old on June 2, 2015. I am reminded that as long as you have someone standing behind you, you can do just about anything. I guess we were poor, but we didn't know it and we didn't see ourselves that way.

Jerome Bell, Brother-in-Law

I grew up in the same neighborhood as the Powell family. I met Glenn's sister when I was twenty-one years-old, and we began dating when she was seventeen. We married four days before she turned eighteen on April 20,1974, and celebrated our forty-second anniversary in 2015. We were born and raised in Toledo Ohio. I was transferred to Jacksonville Florida in 1993. We live in Jacksonville, Florida now. I retired from the railroad in 2015 with forty-four years and now teach tennis and play whenever I get a chance.

The first time I met Glenn, I hated him. He was seven-years old and had this little dog named Peppy. I hated Peppy too. Glenn didn't like to go outside and play, so any chance I got when he was outside, I would rough him up...him and Peppy. I have to admit that after a while he grew on me the more time I spent with him. He had an older brother, but they weren't as close because he was raised by his grandmother. Eventually, I stepped in as a big brother. I started talking to him and teaching him things. Now, I would give him the shirt off my back. He turned out to be a wonderful little brother.

Glenn is driven and smart. He and my wife have that in common. I remember when he got a job cleaning his father's nightclub. He was dedicated and continues to be dedicated to everything he puts his mind to doing. He has this ability to be forceful without being venomous or mean. I think that's why so many people respect him.

While Glenn has always been devoted to his family, he loved everything about the military. When he was younger, I think he was willing to neglect his family to some extent to become successful. As he got older, he realized his family was every bit as important. Many ambitious people experience that.

Glenn was in high school when he told me he was going to the military. I laughed. He was afraid of everything! How would he survive in the military? I told Lauren back then that Glenn was too soft for the military. He shocked me and the rest of his family when he wrote and said it was the best decision he could have made. The military changed Glenn for the better. Now, anything he says he wants to do, I'm one hundred percent behind him and don't doubt that he'll get it done. Glenn is the only person I know that I would loan my car to and it comes back in better shape than when he borrowed it. He would bring it back swept out, detailed and full of gas! I was impressed...lol

Lauren Bell, Glenn's Sister

I'm an author. I have written and published five books. I too followed in my mother's footsteps by working at Kroger for twenty-two years, as many of our family members did, before moving to Florida. Jerome and I have been married for forty-two years and have six children: five girls and one boy. Growing up in a small city like Toledo had a lot great memories as well as its share of bad ones. Our mom was a hard working single parent. We started out living with our grandmother until Mom landed a job at Kroger and she was able to save enough money to move us into a duplex. My older brother wanted to stay with my grandmother, so mom conceded.

Mom was one of the first African Americans to work at Kroger. She worked at the Kroger on Cherry and Bancroft in a predominately polish white neighborhood. She was very fortunate to meet the then Manager Robert Meegan, who took her under his wing, became her friend and watched over her until the day she retired. You didn't run into many people like him back then. He believed in giving people a fair chance, and if you deserved recognition, you were given it. It didn't matter about the color of your skin. Many years later, he hired me. I also believe that he had a hand in helping my mom rise through the ranks to become the first black female manager at Kroger. I remember her telling me that one day, when she was just starting out as a cashier, a white female customer came up to her and asked, 'how did a nigger like you get a job like this?' She didn't know it, but that was her drive to make it, and make it, she did.

As I said, she went on to be a store manager, which put a lot of responsibilities on us, especially me, being the oldest. The first thing is that when we were in the apartment, we had a live in nanny. She took care of us while mom worked. Her name was Miss Sarah. She lived one block from us. Eventually, mom made enough money to purchase her first home. We moved far away from Miss Sarah. She didn't drive, so she had to catch the bus. Eventually, she had to quit because mom's hours made it difficult for her to catch the bus, especially at night. That also shifted a lot of responsibility on me. We basically became latchkey kids. Mom would be gone sometimes when we got up for school. When I got home from school, after doing our homework, I would have to start the preparation for dinner. Mom would come in later and finish it.

One of my fondest memories was on Sundays when we would go pick up my grandmother and drive to Detroit to buy White Castle hamburgers. We would order seventy or eighty hamburgers and we would back the line up! Then we would go to Belle Isle, then back home. On the way home, we stopped in Monroe, Michigan at Independence Ice-Cream store.

Although my mom raised us as a single parent, our dad was very visual, always around. He took very good care of us. Whatever we needed, he provided. We had everything all of the neighborhood kids had and sometimes more. The neighborhood kids would ask why my father was never home, and we would always tell them that he was at work. Where we lived, every house was a two-parent home, so I was very self-conscious about that.

My father owned one of the most popular bar and nightclubs in Toledo. It was The Eureka Social Club and it was located on the corner of Belmont and Forrest. Everybody thought that was a cool thing, so I was proud to say that to my friends. Everybody knew about the Eureka.

As I grew older I started to notice racial tension growing a lot more. There was a lot of activity going on with the Black Panthers. Too young to understand what was going on, but I definitely noticed the tension. My mom would try to explain it, I would watch the news, and of course the word was on the street. We lived only a few blocks from Dorr Street, which was the street that everything was happening on...a very popular spot for prostitutes. Also on Dorr was Dunlap Pool Hall, restaurants, A & P, Kroger, Art's and Clarks Record Shop, Umbles Pharmacy, Carps Clothing, Williards Men Shop, Harry's Men Shop, First National Bank, the World Theatre. You name it, and it was on Dorr Street. The Black Panther Headquarters was even on Dorr Street.

One night this police officer named Miscannon was sitting in his patrol car in front of *The Spot*, which was a restaurant famous for their shrimp and fries. His partner was inside. A man approached the car and shot and killed him. Supposedly a woman in *The Spot* claimed to have seen a man in blues jeans with a black or dark t-shirt or sweatshirt and combat boots, which in the policeman's eyes pointed to a Black Panther. That night—and it went on for days—the police continued to arrest anyone with blue jeans and a dark shirt, young and old. They really didn't take into account any other description. They immediately wanted to blame a Black Panther. From that point on the tension was so high, that I was scared to leave the house, and I certainly didn't go back on Dorr Street for a long time. This came at a time that many cities were rioting—including Toledo—over race related issues.

Glenn was the youngest, so he was very spoiled. I remember when Glenn got so mad at mom because he wanted these shoes and she didn't get them because she said they cost too much. He pouted for days. Over the next few months, Glenn got a job working at the Noble Shoe Store at Swayne Field. He was so happy. Mom was happy too. When he got his first paycheck and he showed it to her. Mom told him that she was taking him to the store to buy those shoes he wanted. He said "Oh no, that's ok, I don't want them now." She said "Oh no, you are buying those shoes, you wanted them when I was paying, so you're going to spend your money to get them!" He was so mad, but he didn't say anything.

His high school friends affectionately called him Monkey Hands because his hands were so big. He even had "MHands" on his license plate. I sent him some kind of monkey birthday card every year! His basement is full of every kind of monkey imaginable. The one thing that he has always loved is red Twizzlers. When he would come home on leave and all of the family members would come over to see him, I would sneak them and pass them out to everybody. He would come in the room and we would all be eating his Twizzlers. He would say Lauri!! I would say "What? I didn't do anything!"

The best thing that ever could have happened to him was that he joined the military. He was so messy before he joined. His bedroom had so many clothes on the floor that you didn't even know what color the carpet was. When he came home on military leave one time, he was folding his clothes and then rolling them up. Everything was neat! Who is this person?

The order and disciplines of military life definitely had a positive influence on him personally as well as professionally. He is a great family man and is very dedicated to his profession wherever he is employed. I am very proud of the way he turned out. I'm also very happy with all of the perks that his career has afforded *me*. I met presidents, been on Air Force One, been places and done things that the general public was unable to experience. So glad I was able to go along for the ride. Love you brother!

Chrystal Harris, First Cousin

Glenn and I are first cousins and he is my favorite. I was born and raised in Toledo as part of the big Powell family. Today, I have a family of my own, which includes my husband, our daughter who serves in the Air Force, and our two sons. My father, Andrew Johnson, was from Georgia, and my mother was born in Toledo. Her father, Tom Powell grew up in Rison, Arkansas. His grandfather, Nick Brewer, was a slave owner, and Tom's grandmother was Mary Brewer. According to oral history, no one in Arkansas—black or white— bothered the Powell children because they were Nick Brewer's grandchildren. Everyone knew it, but it was one of those unspoken secrets. Tom Powell left Arkansas in the early twenties coming to Ohio, which is where he met and married my grandmother, Fannie. The army drafted him, and he fought in WWI. My grandparents had six children. Their third child was my mother, Mildred Powell Johnson. Their fifth child, Margaret Powell, was Glenn's mother. When Tom Powell was alive, he ran his home with an iron fist. He died on a Christmas Eve, and afterwards, Grandma Fannie lived with us for a while.

My first memory of Glenn was of us headed to our grandparent's house when our parents wanted to go out. He and I would play literally all day during those visits. However, at seven in the evening, we had to sit quietly in the living room while grandma Fannie watched her televisions shows: *Hee Haw* and *Lawrence Welk*. Glenn and his family lived on Fernwood on the east side of Detroit Avenue. Our family lived on Oakwood Street. It was so peaceful. Everyone knew everyone. I don't recall any violence in our community when we were growing up. There were dozens of businesses in the community as well: a boxing club, restaurant, corner store, record store, an A&P Grocery store, and two churches. We were never afraid to walk anywhere in the neighborhood. It was a fun place to grow up, and it had plenty of character.

My father worked at the rubber plant around the corner from our house. Glenn's father owned a nightclub called the Eureka Club on Belmont Avenue. On the weekends, Glenn and I would swap turns spending the night at each other's house. He would lay across two chairs eating French fries. Saturday afternoons, we watched "Creature Features" on television and he tried to scare me silly. We all thought Glenn was pretty different. The basement of my house had a drum set. Glenn, his sister Eileen and I would go down to the basement and Glenn would sing and scream at the top of his lungs as he beat on a drum for hours. One night when I went to sleep, he unplugged the lamp, and went under my bed and scared me. One year, my mother hid our Christmas gifts in the attic. Glenn, Eileen, and I went upstairs and found them under a blanket. When Glenn pulled the blanket back, the dolls popped up and he jumped over me, he was so scared. We all ran downstairs.

Though we usually did not attend the same school, we rode the same school bus in high school. When Glenn's friends started calling him Monkey Hands, they started calling me Monkey Hand's cousin. I was still in high school when Glenn left to go to the army.

Glenn is one hundred percent about family. His parents raised him that way. When our mothers, Margaret and Mildred, would go shopping, they would take all of us to dinner and a movie or just on a nice ride. One of the best outings was when they would drive to Columbus and Detroit. We did a lot of family fun stuff. Our parents allowed us to be children. Those times had to have as good an impression on Glenn as they had on me. I think our upbringing made it safe for Glenn to be as ambitious as he was. He is a loyal family man.

Ruth Henderson, Retired Teacher and Cousin

I was born and raised in Toledo, Ohio. I married my husband, Clarence, forty-seven years ago. Clarence was born in Texarkana, Texas, but grew up in Toledo. He went to the military in 1966, and went to work for BP Oil Refinery as an electrician when he returned. He worked there thirty-six years before retiring. I worked for thirty-one years in Toledo's public schools before retiring. My younger sister was closer to Glenn's age; I am quite a bit older.

Clarence and I got to know Glenn and Ronda better after they moved to Washington, D.C. The Toledo area where we grew up was all black. There were very few whites in my graduating class. When I began teaching, I ended up teaching school in the same school district that Glenn and I attended. I always wanted to teach. I taught on the south side of Toledo, which had a large population of Hispanics who transferred to the black schools.

Our parents were hard workers who believed in making sure that their children lived a better life than they had lived. My father also served in the army during World War II as a telephone lineman and went to work at Roberts Rubber Company when he returned. Our grandmother was a homemaker, and my grandfather was a refuse collector. Our family always got together for shopping and going to the movies. All the children would bunch up in the back seat. We were a close family, and to this day we find time to get together. People are always surprised that most of us don't drink or smoke.

We grew up in Greater St. Mary's Church on Belmont Street. We went to Sunday school, and we would remain at church for most of the day. We also attended church almost every day of the week. People thought Glenn's brothers and sisters and mine were siblings. Glenn's mother, aunt Margaret, was a perfectionist and very controlling. If you washed dishes, she demanded that you place all the silverware in the same direction and stack them just right.

I think everyone agreed that Glenn gained a lot from going to the military. The training was definitely good for him. Glenn can be silly and funny, but when it's time to work, he becomes a totally different person. He turns very serious. He's a loving person. The first thing Glenn does when he comes to Toledo is stop off at Rudy's Hot Dog shop. He loves them and says nobody else makes hot dogs the way Rudy's does.

CHAPTER NINETEEN|
The "R" Word

Once you decide to retire, the process and the thoughts about it can be scary and require huge mental adjustments. Depending on how you listen, retirement can tell you that... *you're not the person you once were; you're old and you can't do the things you once did; the person you were for years, and the person that you are now, and the person you are becoming are not the same.* Retirement can get inside your head. It took me a while to accept the fact that retirement, approached from the proper perspective, also opened doors of opportunity to do other things. I wasn't retiring from life but from one part of my life, which was the military. I was still too young to be put out to pasture; however, it was time to turn the page.

Any soldier will tell you that the military is who we are. I grew up in the military, became a man, and learned some of my toughest life lessons in the military. Now, I was being asked to divest myself of that part of me. Once I finally accepted the fact that there was no turning back for me, and that I would wake up the day after my retirement the same person I was the day prior, I jumped into the planning of my celebration party with gusto. Ronda wanted to help me plan the celebration, and she tried. However, she said I was a micromanager and gave up after many failed attempts.

I thought of all the people who had been a part of my life—my wife, my boys, my mother, my siblings, my relatives and best friends, some from childhood. There were members of my work-family who had supported me through thick and thin from the first days of my military career to the years at the White House. When Ronda saw my invitation list, she shook her head in disbelief. She knew that I had met thousands of people over my career, and I rarely lost touch with any of them.

Most of them were contacted and invited. Thankfully, they couldn't all attend. Logistically, that would have been a nightmare.

The Military was hosting the retirement party, but I was choreographing it. After the general invitation list, I moved on to deciding who would speak. The first person on my list would be the most difficult to schedule—Senator Hillary Rodham Clinton. Ever since the 1996 Train Ride, we had forged a friendship and mutual respect. I wanted her there on my special day. I campaigned to get her while still knowing how busy her schedule was.

When the day finally arrived, I was full of jitters. What if no one showed up and the program was a complete flop? To my relief and astonishment, the room began to fill with old and new friends and colleagues. It was a sight to behold. Mark Rosenker, former director, White House Military Office said that few people—the President of the United States, the vice president, and Glenn Powell—could have filled that room. He also admitted later on to everyone that he'd tried to convince me not to retire. It was an amazing night.

I was proud of the letters and tributes that I received, especially from the Presidents: Bush I, Clinton, and Bush II. Secretary Madeleine Albright and former Foreign Advisor, Sandy Berger, sent words of congratulations. Dr. Richard Tubbs, Director of the White House Medical Unit, said the medical team had made me an honorary doctor and that I was the only person who always knew exactly what was going on at 2:00 a.m. The AF1 crew all came up and congratulated me, leaving me with an AF1 blanket. The Secret Service also acknowledged my dedication to our country and devotion to duty.

My mentor and friend Joseph "Jake" Simmons was also in attendance. He mentioned during his presentation that we had traveled around the world together at least three times. I couldn't believe it, but it was true. He truly touched my heart when he said, 'Glenn is someone who takes care of you after you leave AF1. He made his job an art, basically a vocation. You can tell it by the people's lives he impacted.'

To my great honor, Senator Clinton was there in person. She was as elegant and eloquent as ever. She shared President Clinton's well wishes, thanked me for my service to the White House, her family, and the nation. She joked that there should be a special medal named in my honor.

There were several times during the evening—like when my mom and sister spoke—that I nearly lost it emotionally. It was difficult to hold it together as I listened to what others thought about me that night too. I had rarely heard any of my friends or colleagues speak so highly of me. My heart nearly burst to hear how much they genuinely cared for me.

It took me a few days to come down from the high of my retirement celebration. Ronda and I were both blown away by the admiration and love expressed that evening. She said she knew I had lots of friends, but that event proved just what those friends thought of me. I told her I'd be happy to help her plan her retirement party, but—thinking back to my micro-managing ways—she said "absolutely not."

Now, that I'm no longer a part of that elite White House staff, I realize there are a few things I missed out on during my ten years. I never stepped foot in Blair House, which was roughly a block from the White House and the official meeting place of the President and his foreign visitors. The reason may be that the Presidents themselves seldom met there. I never attended a state dinner, though I was invited to one toward the end of the Clinton Administration. It turned out that I was working off campus on the evening of the state dinner. I never bowled in the President' bowling alley located below the press office, or swam in the first family's covered swimming pool. All things considered, somehow this Rust Belt guy from Toledo, Ohio will have to make due with those missed opportunities.

About Glenn W. Powell

Sergeant First Class (Retired) Glenn W. Powell enlisted into the United States Army on April 22, 1982. He completed basic training June 24, 1982, at Fort Dix, New Jersey as a motor vehicle operator, and began his career on August 31, 1982, as a vehicle driver for Bravo Company 502nd Supply & Transportation, Fort Hood, Texas.

In October of 1983, Glenn served as an assistant heavy vehicle driver for Bravo Company, 25th Supply Transportation Battalion, Schofield Barracks, Hawaii. In May 1985, he served as a vehicle driver and training noncommissioned officer for 567th Transportation Company, Fort Eustis, Virginia. On January 25, 1988, he was reassigned to Mannheim Germany where he served as a senior wheel vehicle operator, training noncommissioned officer and squad leader for the 68th Transportation Company, 28th Transportation Battalion. In February of 1990, he was reassigned to the United States and served as a chauffeur and section noncommissioned officer in charge for headquarters company, Intelligence Security Command, Fort Belvoir, Virginia.

Sergeant Powell joined the White House on September 9, 1991, as a chauffeur for the United States Army Transportation Agency. In March of 1992, he served as a transportation coordinator for the White House Press Corps, and in December 1995, assumed the duties of transportation supervisor for Air Force One. Finally, in January 2001, Sergeant Powell was transferred to the White House Military Office, Customer Support and Organizational Development where he served as deputy director.

Sergeant Powell received numerous awards and decorations throughout his service including:

- The Legion of Merit
- The Meritorious Service Medal
- United States Army Commendation Medal with one oak leaf cluster
- Joint Service Achievement Medal United States
- United States Army Achievement Medal with four oak leaf clusters
- Joint Meritorious Unit Award (4th award)
- Driver and Mechanic Badge
- Presidential Service Badge
- United States Army Overseas Ribbon (2nd Award)
- United States Army Service Ribbon
- Noncommissioned Officer Professional Development Ribbon (3rd award)
- National Defense Service Ribbon
- Good Conduct Medals (6th award)

INDEX